The silent cinema

D0631618

Designed by Gillian Greenwood

Liam O'Leary

The silent cinema

*'We are assisting at the birth
of an extraordinary art which has
already found its feet and is destined
for future glories.
The only modern art,
the offspring of the machine
and the human ideal.'*
Louis Delluc, 1919

a dutton vista pictureback
General editor David Herbert

For Ho Chi Yau

© Liam O'Leary 1965
Published in London by Studio Vista Limited
Blue Star House, Highgate Hill, N 19
and in New York by E. P. Dutton and Co Inc
201 Park Avenue South, New York 3, NY
Set in 8pt Univers, 3pts leaded
Made and printed in Great Britain by
Richard Clay (The Chaucer Press), Ltd, Bungay, Suffolk

Contents

◀ AUTUMN MISTS, Dmitri Kirsanoff,
France 1928

Frontispiece
ROMOLA, Henry King, USA 1924
Lillian Gish, MGM

Introduction

The era of the Silent Cinema is a subject of nostalgia for those who lived through it and of curiosity for those who didn't. Individual private collectors of films and national archives across the world share the same sense of discovery, the same wonder and amazement at the rich artistic achievement in this unique period.

The silent cinema has passed away and so it is possible to treat it as a distinct and complete phenomenon. True, a great deal of its characteristics have passed into the sound film but, in spite of many resemblances, it retains its distinction and was something which the sound film by its very definition is not.

The great majority of the public today are not very familiar with silent films. The specialised audiences attending cinemas attached to national film archives and members of film societies are still minority audiences. Occasional use of silent films on television or odd home projections may be the only way in which silent films get seen nowadays. The layman may form his opinions on inferior duplicate copies which lack the sparkle and excellence of the original prints. What he sees may be incomplete survivals or prints based on badly scratched or mutilated copies. The systematic preservation of silent films, inadequate as this may be even today, did not begin until the middle thirties, five years after the silent period had ended. By this time many films had been destroyed and many others had deteriorated. But for a medium which depended above all on the photographed image, it must be stated at once that the pictorial quality of silent films was extraordinarily high and that, before the invention of panchromatic film with its subtler grading of tones and before the modern colour film, the finest camera artists gave their services to this new medium. To anyone privileged to examine original copies of the early one-reel films, the pictorial beauty of the images is a constant source of delight. Nor must we overlook the fact that by the end of the first decade of the century, systems of multicolour hand-tinting and stencil-tinting of the film image had been highly developed and gave a quality to the one-reel film which was most distinctive and inimitable.

We must remember also that the films of the silent era were tinted to emphasise the environment or to heighten the emotional content: blue or green tints for night scenes or marine views, pink for warm scenes of a romantic nature, yellow for interiors.

It is another fallacy that silent films proceeded with jerky move-

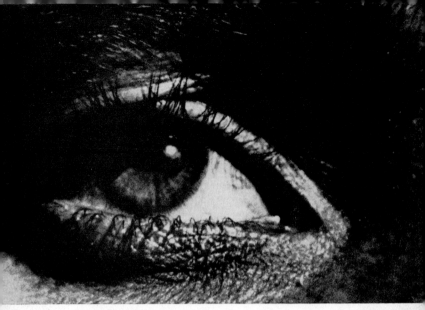

THE MAN WITH THE MOVIE CAMERA,
Dziga Vertov, USSR 1929
The Eye as Hero

ments and that action was speeded up and unnatural. This impression has been created by the projection of silent films on modern machines with a different speed to silent projectors. The truth is that in the teens and twenties of this century audiences were far less sophisticated cinematically and, as film-makers discovered, because of the need for clear registration of movement and the choice of expressive gesture, the tendency was to proceed slowly, so that, in general, silent films flowed along with a stately rhythm which was much more characteristic of the period. True, in some of the comedies speeded-up action gave a greater comic effect, but this was the exception. The point is that silent films were intended to be projected at the speed at which they were photographed. With the coming of the sound film the speed of projectors was increased for purely technical reasons.

The period was one of great ingenuity, experiment and ever-changing variety. It was an era of originality and intense creativity. Because it was new it had to invent its own language. Because it had no tongue it relied on visual action, and it was this which gave it its great beauty and directness of approach. It learned to weld the written word to the moving images. It learned to bend time and space to its needs. It developed a soul.

7

THE FOUR HORSEMEN OF THE APOCALYPSE,
Rex Ingram, USA 1921
On the Pampas, © Metro Pictures Corporation

8

The invention of the cinema

Many diverse discoveries, of course, came together to produce the cinema. The principle of the *camera obscura*, whereby an image of reality is transmitted to the back wall of a darkened box through a tiny hole on the front wall, was discussed as early as 1654 by Athanasius Kircher, a German Jesuit, who also demonstrated the principles of the magic lantern. This engendered the ideas of the photographic camera and the projection lantern. The use of lenses developed the first idea and in the 1820s Niepce succeeded in making the first photograph.

The next stage was to exploit the principle of the persistence of vision. It was discovered that a series of phases of movement projected in rapid succession seemed to merge into one continuous flowing movement. The principle is best demonstrated by those little books where you flip over the pages rapidly and each still picture is linked by the human eye to the next until the illusion of movement is created.

The Zöetrope, or the Wheel of Life, consisted of a revolving band containing within its wall a series of action phases; while on the outside of the band, above the position of the pictures, were slots through which one viewed the pictures as they revolved. This produced the illusion of movement. The Belgian Joseph Plateau is mainly associated with this particular discovery and many were the devices which exploited the principle.

1878 was the year of Eadweard Muybridge's photographic experiments at Palo Alto in California. A series of cameras set up and operated by a series of trip wires photographed a varied number of movements by a horse. Muybridge extended his experiments to analysing the movements of naked men, women and children, movements of men on horseback, wrestlers etc. These series of pictures aroused considerable interest among artists, particularly in Paris where Etienne Jules Marey was carrying on similar experiments, with a difference. Whereas Muybridge used many cameras, Marey was aiming at a single camera-gun which would record all the phases, and in 1882 he constructed the Chronophotographe. It is possible that the term 'shooting' originates from Marey's invention.

In 1878 Edison patented the Phonograph. Sound recording was

Zöetrope Band of Movement Phases

now a practical reality. Edison really wanted talkies. He wanted to have moving pictures to accompany his records. This led him into the world of moving pictures.

Photography relied on sensitised glass plates in its early stages. Celluloid was found to be a more satisfactory and flexible base. In 1884 the Eastman Dry Plate and Film Company was founded. At first sensitised paper was used, but in 1888 the Company was using celluloid.

In 1888 Emile Renaud found it possible to project pictures from his invention of 1876, the Praxinoscope. This came very near to looking like the Cinematograph, as it used a band of images perforated between the pictures for movement purpose. The pictures were drawn images, not photographed reality. A series of reflecting mirrors helped to produce the illusion of movement. It was now a matter of setting the photographed images like those of Marey and Muybridge in motion and using the flexible celluloid film.

From 1889 events moved rapidly. Edison and Dickson, his assistant and in many ways the brain behind the new invention, were taking pictures with their camera, the Kinetograph, and significantly using film 35 mm wide. In the same year their first sound film appeared. In 1890 their Kinetoscope machine made it possible to view through a narrow hole a continuous chain of moving-picture scenes. These machines were put on the market and the first phase of the cinema was under way. The first film studio, known as 'The Black Maria', was constructed in 1894 on Edison's property at West Orange, and here the first commercial films for the Kinetoscope were made. There was Fred Ott in his classical sneeze, Annabella the dancer, one of many such, the famous Annie Oakley in her shooting act, the great Sandow revealing his chest expansion, dances of the Sioux Indians, etc.

It is impossible in a short survey to detail the people who made

significant or less successful contributions to the development of the cinema at this stage. The names of Louis Aimé le Prince and William Friese-Greene of England, Georges Demeny of France, Ottomar Anschütz and Max Skladanowski of Germany must also be mentioned, and the Americans Eugene Lauste and Acme le Roy. It is significant that the French pioneer film-makers Louis and Auguste Lumière, Leon Gaumont and Charles Pathé were all involved with the cinema before 1895.

To exploit the Kinetoscopes of Edison, Kinetoscope Parlours were opened in the principal cities of America in 1894. The race was now on for the projection on a screen of the films already in existence. The brothers Latham and W. K. L. Dickson, who had parted company with Edison, marketed a Panoptikon which could project films. In Europe the Kinetoscope was launched in London and Paris. In London Robert William Paul was responsible for their manufacture, and in the following year these were bought for France by Charles Pathé.

We now approach the generally accepted date for the true beginning of the cinema as we know it. Louis and Auguste Lumière, whose photographic factory was situated at Lyons, had been taking films from the beginning of the year with their special apparatus. On 28th September 1895, the first projection of films to a paying audience was given at the Grand Café, Boulevard des Capucines, Paris, a truly historic occasion.

Edison had found a means of projection when he took over Armat's apparatus and gave it the name of Edison Vitascope. The first public projection with this apparatus took place in New York in Koster and Bial's Music Hall. In the meantime, the Lumière programme had travelled to the Empire Theatre, London, and in the same city Robert Paul gave his first public performances at Olympia. The cinema was now under way.

The Magic Lantern

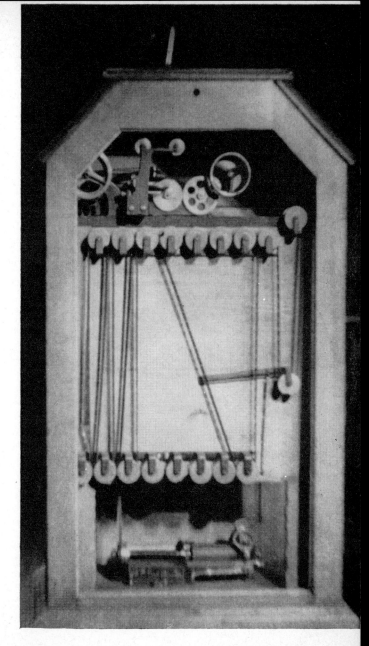

An Edison Kinetoscope

The First Film Studio

The age of the one reel film, 1895–1913

There was an urgency about the making of some of these early films. Many of the pioneers feared that the novelty of seeing the world on the screen might wear off, and that it was important to make money while the sun still shone. When a young man called Georges Méliès, who ran the Théâtre Robert Houdin, approached one of the Lumières and expressed his interest in films, he got the rather discouraging reply: 'Young man, my invention is not for sale, and in any case it would only ruin you. Perhaps for a time it may be exploited as a scientific curiosity, but apart from that it has no commercial future whatever.' But he was obviously not talking to the right man, for Georges Méliès persisted; he did business with Robert Paul, made and showed films at his theatre and, in May, 1897, built his film studio at Montreuil. Perhaps Méliès was the sign the new industry needed, because he brought the light of his fertile imagination to bear on the new medium and continued to produce marvels the like of which had never before been seen. He was quick to seize upon all the tricks possible to the camera whereby time and space could be manoeuvred for artistic ends. For him the camera was a magic wand. On the screen people appeared and disappeared in a trice, magic transformations took place, people travelled to the moon, to the North Pole, to the depths of the sea or wherever Méliès' fancy took him. His were the first great fantasies of the cinema—films like *The Bewitched Inn* (1897), *The Brahmin and the Butterfly* (1901), *The Voyage Across the Impossible* (1904), *Soap Bubbles* (1906), *The Conquest of the Pole* (1912) and hundreds of others which gave joy to past generations and still keep their creative freshness and individuality. Méliès, who also made documentary films and historic reconstructions such as *The Dreyfus Affair* (1899) and *The Coronation of Edward VII* (1902), was the film's first *metteur en scène* in that he planned, designed the scenery and effects and directed all the operations at his studio. He was born in Paris in 1861. In his days of success he issued his films under the trade mark of Star Films. In 1911 he accepted help from Pathé, who became his distributor. By 1913 he had ceased to make films and was hopelessly in debt. After the First World War his theatre and studios were sold. In 1923 he accepted a job running a toy shop in the Montparnasse Station. In 1929 a tardy tribute was paid to him: he received the Cross of the Legion of Honour and finished

KOSTER & BIAL'S MUSIC HALL

Thirty-fourth Street, Herald Square.

KOSTER, BIAL & CO., • • • • **Proprietors**
   ALBERT BIAL, • • • **Sole Manager.**
W. A. McConnell, • • • • **Business Manager.**

Week Commencing Monday Evening, April 20, 1896.

Evenings, 8:15   Saturday Matinee, 2:15

THIS PROGRAMME is subject to alterations at the discretion of the management.

1	OVERTURE,	"Masaniello,"	Auber

2   **WM. OLSCHANSKY**
The Russian Clown

3   **CORA CASELLI**
Eccentric Dancer.

4   **THE THREE DELEVINES**
In their original act "Satanic Gambols".

5   **PAULINETTI and PICO**
The Athletic Gymnast and Gymnastic Comedian.

MONS. and MME.
6   **DUCREUX-GERALDUC**
French Duettists.

7   **THE BROTHERS HORN**
Assisted by MISS CHARLOTTE HALLETT
"London Life."

THOMAS A. EDISON'S LATEST MARVEL

8   # THE VITASCOPE,

Presenting selections from the following:

"Sea Waves," "Umbrella Dance," "The Barber Shop," "Burlesque Boxing," "Monroe Doctrine," "A Boxing Bout," "Venice, showing Gondolas," "Kaiser Wilhelm, reviewing his troops," "Skirt Dance," "Butterfly Dance," "The Bar Room," "Cuba Libre."

INTERMISSION 10 MINUTES

IN THE GRAND PROMENADE
Dr. Leo Sommer's Blue Hungarian Band.

Programme continued on next page.

The Vitascope opens at Koster and Bial's Music Hall, New York

his days in a home in the environs of Paris, where he died on the 21st January 1938.

The first efforts of the early film-makers might be divided into three categories. One consisted of actuality films, recording topical events, visits to strange places and other exotic phenomena, and taking advantage of the travels of cameramen. Their main purpose was broadly educational, but they also exploited pictorial romanticism to the utmost and many of these films are very attractive to look at today.

Another was that of the popular trick film which consisted of action run backwards, people being decapitated by motor-cars, transformations and disappearances.

The third comprised comedy films—mainly slapstick with an element of the chase. Jean Durant specialised in this film style in the Calino series. *Calino Jerry-builder* (1911), for example, shows a badly built house collapsing and every possible bit of fun is extracted from this situation. In *Calino's Boarders* (1911) an explorer's trunks are opened by a servant and lions emerge, creating havoc about the house. André Deed, known to the Italians as Cretinetti and to us as Foolshead, made a series of films in which he covered nearly every comic situation and for his efforts began to command over twenty thousand dollars a month.

The animated or cartoon film had its earliest exponent in Emile Cohl, an innovator whose story had a sad ending since he finished his career on the Paris streets selling newspapers. His *Phantasmagorie* (August, 1908), *Drama Amongst the Puppets* (November, 1908) and *The Joyous Microbes* (April, 1909) are the ancestors of every cartoon since, from *Mutt and Jeff, Felix* and *Bonzo* to Disney.

While the houses of Pathé and Gaumont were the powers in France, new industrial set-ups were taking place in America. In May, 1897, the American Mutoscope and Biograph Company took over from the American Mutoscope Company, and in November Wallace McCutcheon filmed *Rip Van Winkle* with the famous actor Joseph Jefferson, the first time a well-known player appeared in a film. The same year John Stuart Blackton and Albert Smith formed the Vitagraph Company, filming their first effort on the roof of the Morton Building, New York. Thus two major American Companies who were to contribute much to the cinema in the coming years were now in existence.

Edison, who was very jealous of his patents, kept relentless watch on companies who in any way infringed his monopoly of

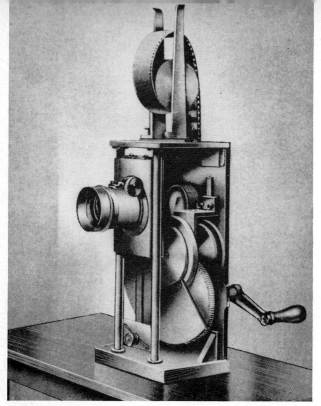

An Early Lumière Projector

apparatus. In 1902 his new director, Edwin Porter, made *The Life of an American Fireman* and followed it up the next year with an even more famous film, *The Great Train Robbery*. This showed a marked improvement on anything which had been done so far in the way of story narration, with scenes split up into more natural arrangements. At this early stage of film-making, many problems remained to be solved if the most effective use was to be made of the camera. The film-maker had to choose the order of items which he was to present, and obviously it was not much use presenting them any old how, or relying on the printed title to get one out of a continuity mess. It was not long before it was found that the camera could be made to move both laterally and vertically on its stand in order to follow the movement of its object, or it could be put on a moving vehicle to record what it saw. The camera could move close in on a subject, or it could take a distant view of events. Instinctively many film-makers realised these things, and, as competition was very keen, they kept an eye on what their rivals were doing so that a refinement here or there did not go unnoticed. Constantly in these early films one is surprised to see effects which have been credited to later filmmakers, particularly to Griffith and to the Germans.

At first the draw of the cinema was its tremendous novelty, and it found its home where novelties are usually exploited—fairgrounds and penny gaffs—and nobody seriously considered it as of any consequence. Then, with the improvements in techniques and the multiplication of its wonders, it moved into the small halls or Nickelodeons as they were called in America. Audiences flocked to these halls and contracted the cinema habit and, as the players and companies became known and advertising gave more

American Biograph Studio
at 11 East 14th Street, New York in 1908

Méliès' Studio at Montreuil

information about the film and its making, audiences' interest increased. In 1913 it was estimated that there were sixty thousand cinemas in the world of which more than a quarter were in America. Films were an international business. To cross a frontier the only change needed was to have the sub-titles translated. International stars became known from country to country. In Britain, for instance, Asta Nielsen of Denmark and Henny Porten of Germany were popular stars. Italian players like Bertini, Borelli or Amleto Novelli became household words. New films were eagerly awaited and, when the day of the serial film came, it was almost a dereliction of religious duty if a chapter were missed. By now the players were well known to film-goers. Mary Pickford, Charlie Chaplin, Mabel Normand, Florence Turner, Jack Kerrigan, John Bunny, Maurice Costello, Clara Kimball Young, Gene Gauntier all meant something to the public. It was not mere enthusiasm which bound players to audience. It was more like a love relationship.

In America two major companies, Biograph and Vitagraph, supplied a large number of one-reel films. Biograph's main claim to fame was its employment of an actor called David Wark Griffith, who had distinctive talents and heaps of good old Victorian sentiment. He was born in La Grange, Oldham County, Kentucky, on 22nd January, 1875. He had ambitions to be a dramatist and tended to despise the new-fangled cinema. But an artist must eat, and once in as director of movies Mr Griffith set about making a thorough job of it. With the help of a clever camera-

NAPOLEON, J. Stuart Blackton, USA 1906
William Humphreys and Julia Swayne Gordon

THE CONQUEST OF THE POLE, Georges Méliès, France 1912
Design by Méliès

man called Billy Bitzer, he tried everything once. His subjects ranged from Leo Tolstoy to hillbilly comedy, from Ibsen to social indictments by Frank Norris, and never far round the corner were treacly sentimental dramas of Victorian origin. His thinking was as woolly as his technique was brilliant. He moulded his actors for the screen with the greatest care, he experimented with lighting, he carried the film in his head so that there were no scenario-writers to take the credit and, above all, he specialised in the American War type of film which was so near to him and his Southern traditions. His influence on the cinema was tremendous, in that he consistently sought after and discovered methods of filming which were analysed and adopted in more conscious ways by the Russian film-makers of the twenties; but of course he was to influence American film-making too.

At this time film production in America was centred in and about New York, and Hollywood hadn't even been heard of. In 1910, however, Griffith went to California where the Selig Company

John Bunny, the first great comedian

had opened a studio in 1909. After that he made several trips to the West but returned time and again to film in the New York area.

The Vitagraph Company followed a less spectacular course. Their films were produced with taste and care and they were served by excellent and experienced players. Comedies of ordinary life, a series of Napoleonic dramas with William Humphries and Julia Swayne Gordon, the John Bunny and Flora Finch comedies, a series of Shakespeare dramas, a lengthy *Life of Moses* (1908), an *Uncle Tom's Cabin* (1910), and a three-reel version of *A Tale of Two Cities* (1911), these were some of their achievements.

FROM THE MANGER TO THE CROSS,

Their players, Maurice Costello, the first film-matinée idol, Florence Turner, their great dramatic star, the comedians John Bunny and Flora Finch, players like Norma Talmadge, Lilian Walker, Clara Kimball Young, Charles Kent and Antonio Moreno, were well known and appreciated. Many famous personalities of the film industry played with this company, including Rex Ingram and Rudolph Valentino.

In 1908 the Kalem Company was formed by George Klein, Frank Marion from Edison and Samuel Long, a former Edison representative. One of their first films was *Ben Hur* (1908),

Sidney Olcott, USA 1913, Kalem

Edwin S. Porter, a pioneer director

Mabel Normand, a brilliant comedienne ▶

directed by Sidney Olcott. This director had a theory that stories should be filmed in their actual location, and in 1909 he visited Ireland and made popular patriotic dramas like *Rory O'More, Ireland the Oppressed, The Colleen Bawn,* and *Arrah na Pogue.* Later he visited fifteen other countries and returned with films notable for their fine local colour. His most famous film was *From the Manger to the Cross* (1913), shot in Palestine.

Other American companies of this period were Essanay, who introduced the famous Bronco Billy Anderson, the first of the cowboy stars, Lubin, Selig, Thanhouser, Imp, American, Majestic, Reliance and Kay-Bee.

THE ABYSS, Hjalmar Davidsen and Urban Gad, Denmark 1911
Asta Nielsen

In England, there emerged the work of pioneers such as Robert Paul, Cricks and Martin, Cecil Hepworth and the Brighton School which consisted of G. Albert Smith and James Williamson. Although the latter group had a short life in films, its contribution was remarkable. Georges Sadoul in his *Pioneers of the Cinema* thought fit to devote a chapter to its work. He concludes: 'The Brighton School is most remarkable because it introduced to the cinema montage, the chase, simultaneous action, a certain social realism and the open air setting. With Smith and Williamson the English were the first to break the glass cage which Méliès pretended to have enclosed the scene.'

Cecil Hepworth, whose activities continued into the twenties, made his mark with the classic *Rescued by Rover* in 1905. He was responsible for films with a truly English flavour and produced a wide range of films exploiting the English rural scene. His leading ladies, Chrissie White and Alma Taylor, had tremendous popularity with the public and were to him what the Gishes were to Griffith.

Nearly every European country had its production going by this time. The period of the one-reeler (although longer films had been made) was characterised by the tremendous variety of these short subjects. Competition was keen and film-makers looked around for new subjects. The classics were plundered. Shakespeare stories were drawn upon, myths, legends and popular folk-tales were used. Crime stories brushed shoulders with the works of Hugo, Dickens, Zola, Eugène Sue and Victorien Sardou. New social ideas crept into the films. There seemed to be a need to expand the story length, and this is precisely what happened.

The arrival of the feature film, 1913–14

The one-reel film had been an ideal training ground for the early artists of the cinema. Griffith is the perfect example of this, and it is not without significance that the two talented Swedes, Victor Sjöström and Mauritz Stiller, were able to see his films in Stockholm theatres before they joined Swedish Biograph in 1911. Giovanni Pastrone directed the one-reel comedies of André Deed for his Itala Company. From the ranks of actors in one-reel films came a host of important directors—men like Rex Ingram, Frank Borzage, James Cruze, Robert Z. Leonard. Many cameramen, too, got their first knowledge of the cinema in this way.

By 1913 the feature film had arrived. Just as the length of a film increased, so did the size of the subject, and the Italians were largely responsible for this. They virtually invented the spectacle film. As early as 1910 Giovanni Pastrone made a *Fall of Troy* in three reels. It was on a lavish scale and was singularly impressive. The year before, Giuseppe de Liguoro exploited trick-photography in his version of *The Inferno*. And in 1912 Enrico Guazzoni made *Quo Vadis* which he followed in 1913 with *Mark Antony and Cleopatra* and *Caius Julius Caesar* in 1914. The players may have been portly and theatrical but the scale of production with its marching armies, chariot races and elaborate arena scenes was

CABIRIA, Giovanni Pastrone, Italy 1913

something the public had never known before and was certainly something that the theatre could not provide. This was spectacle before Cecil B. de Mille, and it set a pattern for Italian films for years to come.

In 1914 Gabriele d'Annunzio expressed the view that 'the cinema must give to the spectators fantastic visions, lyric catastrophes, marvels born of the most sturdy imagination; as in the epic poems it must bring back the marvellous, the super-marvellous of today and tomorrow'. It is unlikely that he was disappointed with Pastrone's epic *Cabiria* (1913), although his association with the film was not as extensive as the publicity led one to believe. The unity of the work is delicately held and the magnificence of the action never swamps the human interest of the characters. It is a tale of the Punic Wars. Opening in Sicily with an eruption of Mount Etna, it follows the fortunes of the little Cabiria, who is captured by pirates and taken to Carthage where she is to undergo sacrifice to Moloch. Her story is interwoven with the larger historical events taking place. The film is full of great moments: the crossing of the Alps by Hannibal, the Siege of Syracuse and the destruction of Massinissa's army. Incidentally no hero has ever had such a wonderful introduction to an audience as Massinissa; Sophonisba's maid's sub-title reads: 'He is like a wind from the desert bringing the scent of dust and lions and the message of Astarte.' The film is not least remarkable for its complete poetic fusion of sub-title and image. The staging and settings are very fine, the acting (with one exception) superb and the camerawork of Segundo de Chomon, with its most sensitive moving camera, a model of imagination and discretion. It is hard to believe that this film did not influence Griffith in *Intolerance.*

But not all Italian films were spectacles. Negroni's charming *Story of a Pierrot* (1913) with Francesca Bertini, *Lost in the Dark* (1914) by Nino Martoglio with Giovanni Grasso, *Assunta Spina* (1915) by Gustavo Serena with Bertini, and *Ashes* (1916) by Febo Mari with the great Duse herself, were films of quite a different calibre, the ancestors of neo-realism perhaps.

There was another type of Italian film which was absorbing the energies of the female stars that Italy seemed able to create most readily. It was the era of the *diva*. Francesca Bertini has already been mentioned. Then came Lyda Borelli, Pina Menichelli, Soava Gallone, Maria Jacobini and Hesperia. To set them off there were the dramas of Dumas Fils and Sardou.

Two films of 1916 were unusual: *Perfidious Spell* by Anton

SALOME, J. Gordon Edwards, USA 1918
Theda Bara, Fox

Giulio Bragaglia with its strange futuristic patterns (the first avant-garde film?) and *The Kings, the Castles and the Bishops* directed by I. Illuminati with a script by Lucio D'Ambra.

Many established actors had by now taken to films and were regarding the hitherto despised cinema with a favourable eye. But not all were equally successful. In 1913 Sarah Bernhardt had made a *Queen Elizabeth* and failed utterly to understand the medium in which she was working. Her theatrical flamboyance, effective as it may have been in the theatre, produced a merely comic effect on film, whereas Duse with her intense inner quality of restraint is very moving to watch and anticipates the modern

31

Pearl White, Queen of the American Serials

methods of acting for the screen. Other famous actors such as le Bargy, Minnie Maddern Fiske, Rejane, Mounet Sully, Frank Benson and Johnson Forbes Robertson acted on films, the latter appearing in a version of *Hamlet* made by the Hepworth Company in Britain in 1913.

In May, 1909, Charles Magnusson founded the Swedish Biograph Company. With his brilliant cameraman Julius Jaenzen, possibly the best in the world, he launched into production and was a knowledgeable and experienced film-maker when he engaged Victor Sjöström and Mauritz Stiller, both graduates of the theatre. Sjöström had paid a flying visit to the Pathé Studios in Paris, and Stiller was fired by his interest in a Vitagraph film. These were the architects of a truly national cinema and two of the most sophisticated directors the cinema has ever known. Their first work consisted of sensational crime dramas, often banned by the censor, but gradually they found their direction. The Swedish

Cinema was a cinema of the great outdoors. The acting was refined and naturalistic and the style sprang directly from Swedish environment and temperament. Of his beginnings Sjöström writes : 'I had the great fortune to be allowed to direct films at a time when both they and I were young. I was then an actor on the stage, I loved the stage and I had a great contempt for this newcomer that was called Film. So I made up my mind to try to change it thoroughly, try to lift it up to a higher level—probably youth and vanity sailing in the same boat. And as luck would have it my films from *Ingeborg Holm* onward made money for the company and I was allowed to have my own way.'

Ingeborg Holm, made in 1913, was a key film. This was the story of a poor woman whose husband had died and left her in debt with two small children. The children are taken from her and she is sent to a workhouse. The separation causes a mental breakdown. One of the children dies and the other becomes a

A DAUGHTER OF THE GODS,
Herbert Brenon, USA 1916, Fox

sailor. Treated by a sympathetic young doctor she is eventually reunited with her son. The principal role, played with restraint and understanding by Hilda Borgström, was deeply moving. To compare this performance with Bernhardt's in *Queen Elizabeth* underlines the fundamental differences between stage and screen acting. Sjöström's sensitive relation of people to their environment was beautifully shown in the sequence where Ingeborg escapes from the workhouse and goes to the farmhouse where her child is ill. The true language of the screen has never been so lucid.

Stiller was born in Finland. He was a man of elegant and refined tastes and his approach to films was perhaps more aesthetic than that of Sjöström. Again, his early films were melodramatic, but in treatment they worked towards a quality which was distinctively Swedish and very sensitive.

In Denmark, at one time one of the largest film-producing countries in the world, Ole Olsen had founded his Nordisk Company and made his first story film in 1904. For him Viggo Larsen made the famous *Marriage Under the Revolution* in 1909. Prior to this Nordisk had turned out the usual spate of classical stories: *Trilby, Dr Jekyll and Mr Hyde, Madame Sans Gêne, The Borgias* and an adaptation of Strindberg's *Dance of Death*. As the company developed, many fine directors like Alfred Lind, also a cameraman, August Blom, Robert Dinesen, Benjamin Christensen and Hjalmar Davidsen, came to the fore, while actors like Asta Nielsen, Clara Pontoppidan, Betty Nansen, Waldemar Psilander, Olaf Fönss and Robert Dinesen became known throughout the world. The Danish films specialised in passion and intrigue and in crime and detection. Certain films, of course, were outside these categories. Lind and Dinesen made *The Four Devils* in 1911, a story of circus people that was a resounding success. And when Gerhardt Hauptman's novel *Atlantis* was directed by August Blom, its sensational scenes of a liner sinking in mid-Atlantic made the name Nordisk a household word. The appearance of Asta Nielsen in Blom's *Ballet Dancer* (1911) was another feather in Nordisk's cap because she was one of the best-known European actresses of her day; and her *The Abyss*, made by Hjalmar Davidsen and Urban Gad in the same year, confirmed the impression she had already made. The tormented dramas of Holger Madsen with their exotic and morbid stories were also characteristic of the Danish cinema of this time. *The Spirits* and *The Evangelist* of 1914 were the most outstanding, and in the latter Waldemar Psilander gave a remarkable performance. Benjamin Christensen's spy drama of

1913, *The Mysterious X*, marked the appearance of yet another Danish talent. All these films, because of the high quality of their production, acting and direction, were readily accepted abroad.

France continued her production during these years. Léonce Perret's *Child of Paris* (1913) indicates the fine standards of film-making that prevailed. The feeling for reality and environment is particularly well represented in this story of crooks and kidnapping, and the film has an interest far beyond that of its subject. Jasset, whose early death finished a promising career, made further serial films, a branch of cinema most strikingly developed by Louis Feuillade. *Zigomar the Eelskin* and *Protea* of Jasset in 1913 gave way to Feuillade's first famous *Fantomas* series of the same year. Feuillade was master of this form. All the exciting adventures involved in the conflict between the master-mind and the clever criminal were raised to a level of poetry. Feuillade's films with their use of natural locations and heavily characterised

Fatty Arbuckle, the tragic comedian

interiors make fascinating viewing today, floating continually as they do into sheer fantasy which resembles that of Bunuel.

Also interesting in the French cinema of this time was the rise of Max Linder, the first great comedian of the screen. This elegant mimic adventurer seemed to anticipate all the qualities which one associates with Chaplin and Fairbanks. He had sang-froid, panache and all the characteristics which are supposed to be peculiarly French. Prior to 1910 he had appeared in a series of films, but in that year his screen type became fixed and the ebullient little dandy achieved an enormous success with the public. In 1911 he made *Max and the Quinquina*, in 1912 *A Farm Idyll* and in 1913 *Max Toreador*.

In America also comedy was booming. In 1913 Mack Sennett engaged Charles Chaplin, a British comedian with Fred Karno's company, 'Mumming Birds'. At Keystone Sennett had gathered around him a brilliant group of zany comics including Ford Sterling, Fatty Arbuckle, Mack Swain, Al St John, Marie Dressler and Mabel Normand. His vigorous slapstick style extracted the maximum impact from custard-pie throwing and breath-taking chases. His famous Keystone Cops and Bathing Beauties were another feature of his work. This school of comedy was a nursery for talent and its graduates included Gloria Swanson, Harry Langdon, Phyllis Haver, Marie Prevost and Carole Lombard. The studios were situated at Glendale, California. In adding Chaplin to his group he was to launch one of the most spectacular careers.

By 1913 Cecil B. de Mille, an actor and playwright, and his colleagues Jesse Lasky and Samuel Goldwyn, founded the Jesse L. Lasky Feature Play Company and headed for Hollywood, where they produced *The Squaw Man* (1913) in an old barn on the corner of Vine Street and Sunset Boulevard. This was the start of the Paramount Company, and all its founders were to play a big role in the American cinema. Around this time Adolph Zukor had founded his Famous Players Company, inspired by the appearance of Bernhardt in *Queen Elizabeth*, a film which he exploited in America. He engaged well-known stage players. Edwin Porter's *Eternal City* (1915) featured Pauline Frederick, and James Hackett starred in Hugh Ford's *Prisoner of Zenda* (1913). The year 1913 also saw the entry of William Fox into film production. He was to be a major figure of the twenties.

The serial film in America followed the examples of Jasset and Feuillade. The great Albert Capellani production of *Les Miserables* (1912) which ran in four parts must also have promoted the idea

THE FUGITIVE, Reginald Barker, USA 1914
William S. Hart

of serials. In the same year Selig Pictures made *The Adventures of Kathlyn* with Kathlyn Williams in eighteen episodes based on a series running in the Chicago Herald Tribune. Next year came Edison's *Dolly of the Dailies* with Mary Fuller, Pathé Exchange's *Perils of Pauline* and Thanhouser's *Million Dollar Mystery*.

In Germany, as early as 1902, Oskar Messter and Franz Porten had formed the Messter Film Company. Their most famous star was Franz Porten's daughter Henny, a versatile player who achieved world fame and has remained an important player in German films up to the present day. In 1913 a young Danish director, Stellan Rye, made *The Student of Prague* with Paul Wegener and his wife Lyda Salmonova. This story of a young man who sold his soul to the Devil was a characteristic German theme. Characteristic also were the talents which collaborated in its making. The settings for the film were designed by Dr Hans Poelsig, the brilliant theatre

Charles Chaplin and Max Linder

designer, and the film was largely shot in Prague with its medieval
streets and an old Jewish cemetery. The camera-work was by
Guido Seeber. Unlike the German films to come, which were
particularly products of the hothouse atmosphere of the studio,
Wegner's film had a feeling for nature.

What was to be a tragic prophecy was *Cursed be War* (1913)
made by Alfred Machin. This anticipated the horrors of the coming
holocaust. His scenes of fighting on land and in the air seem im-
possibly ironic to us today. On a purely production scale this film
also appears remarkable in its sweeping panoramas of war in
action, and stands up very well in comparison with the later *Four
Horsemen of the Apocalypse* (1921) and *The Big Parade* (1925).
By 1914 the First World War had begun.

The war years, 1914–18

While the war raged in Europe another battle was being planned in America. D. W. Griffith, who had been steadily consolidating his position and increasing his mastery of the cinema, had begun work on his epic *Birth of a Nation* which received its world première at Clunes Auditorium, Los Angeles, on 8th February 1915. Previously Griffith had handled large-scale fighting scenes in *The Battle* (1911) and in *The Massacre* (1915). In 1913 he completed his first large-scale four-reel film, *Judith of Bethulia*, in answer to the Italian spectacles.

To *Birth of a Nation*, however, he brought all his resources and ambitions and he handled every aspect of production himself. He raised the money, one hundred and ten thousand dollars, (an enormous sum for those days), he visualised the sweep of the film,

INTOLERANCE, D. W. Griffith, USA 1916 ▶
The Palace of Belshazzar

BIRTH OF A NATION, D. W. Griffith, USA 1914
Henry B. Walthall and Miriam Cooper

D. W. Griffith directing

designed it, directed it and organised it. There was no detailed scenario to guide him, for he carried the whole project in his head. He worked on the film from July 1914 to October of the same year. With a running time of two and three-quarter hours, it contained one thousand, three hundred and seventy-five shots.

The story mingles the adventures of two pairs of lovers with the larger events of the American Civil War—the battles, the assassination of Lincoln, the degradation of the South, the arrogance of the freed negroes, the carpet-baggers and the rise of the Ku Klux Klan. The film is projected from a strongly biased Southern viewpoint and this led to much protest and even riots in cinemas where it was shown. It is doubtful if Griffith fully understood the implications of what he was saying in the film, but he stoutly defended it and followed up with his plea for understanding, *Intolerance* (1916).

The world success of *Birth of a Nation* was a foregone conclusion. Its great battle scenes had the authenticity of the Matthew Brady photos of the actual war. The carefully chosen settings and variety of locations from all over California, and the brilliance of a cast headed by Henry B. Walthall as the Little Colonel, Lillian Gish as Elsie Stoneman and Mae Marsh as Flora Cameron, was bound to make an impact. Its presentation in regular theatres at high prices did much to give the cinema a new status and prestige.

Parallel action to create exciting climaxes, cameras moved from long-distant panoramas to close-ups for details, careful selection of incident, rhythmical editing of sequences, all these contributed to a new language of screen storytelling and influenced the shape of films to come, particularly those from Russia. Griffith earned one million dollars in the first year. In succeeding years the film was to earn over twenty million dollars.

Five of its players, Raoul Walsh, Joseph Henabery, Elmer Clifton, Donald Crisp and Erich von Stroheim became important directors. Wallace Reid was to become the great matinée idol. Elmo Lincoln was to be the first Tarzan, and nearly all its players became stars or featured players in the years to come.

THE SONG OF THE RED FLOWER,
Mauritz Stiller, Sweden 1918
Lars Hanson and Grete Almroth, Svenska

ANJUTA THE DANCER, Mauritz Stiller, Sweden 1916
Lars Hanson, Richard Lund and Jenny Hasselquist, Svenska

Griffith now had another project up his sleeve. Stung by the attacks on him for his implied hostility to negroes and his championship of the Ku Klux Klan, he visualised a great film devoted to the theme of international goodwill and brotherhood, showing how, when these principles are laid aside, injustice and hatred sow their evil seeds. He called his film *Intolerance* and again made it outside the pale of the Hollywood set-up, raising the money himself from private sources as well as from the receipts of *Birth of a Nation*. Originally one of the episodes was planned as a separate film. This was the modern story, *The Mother and the Law*, but now he conceived the idea of running this parallel with three other stories—the death of Christ at the hands of the Pharisees, the massacre of the Huguenots in 16th-century France and the destruction of Babylon by the Persians in 539 BC. The modern story dealt with class hatred and modern injustices. These stories were to develop together on the screen, switching from one to the other and working to a dramatic multiple climax with the Crucifixion, the slaughter of the Huguenots and the death of Belshazzar; but in the modern story a happy ending is permitted, the hero being rescued from the scaffold. The film ends with an epilogue showing the millennium, while throughout the film interludes of a woman rocking a cradle echo the thoughts of Walt Whitman. By now Griffith was working in terms of symphonic proportions and the result is a monument to his unbounded ambitions.

The project was tremendous and as usual Griffith carried the whole burden of the effort: independent finance and a vision which existed in his mind—never on paper—colossal sets, sixty thousand extras, the most complex story ever told on the screen, this was just some of the material to be moulded into a co-ordinated whole. The film cost one and three-quarter million dollars. It was made under conditions of great secrecy. Hollywood didn't quite know the significance of all the great structures which were being run up near Hollywood and Sunset Boulevards. Some work had been done on the film in 1914, but it was not until June, 1915, that Griffith went all out on production. It seems a miracle that Griffith was able to edit it in two months, but he had a clear picture in his head during shooting, so that he knew where each shot fitted in.

It had its première in the Liberty Theatre, New York, on the 5th September, 1916. Its running time was three hours and thirty-five minutes. The impact of the film on audience and critics was extraordinary. The creative sweep of the work made people think in terms of Shakespeare and Beethoven. Crowned heads, writers and artists all paid tribute to its grandeur and artistic merits, but it did not achieve the financial success of its predecessor. The demands it made on audience receptivity were enormous. The film was really ahead of its time. In Europe, however, it had much more appreciation. Its influence on other film-makers, notably Eisenstein, was profound.

The cast of *Intolerance* runs to four pages and reads like a *Who's Who* of Hollywood, with such exotic names as Ruth St Denis and Sir Herbert Beerbohm Tree thrown in for good measure. The energetic Griffith, in the middle of preparation for his epic subjects, also found time to supervise and script a large series of films for the Triangle Company and so helped to mould less-experienced

BARNABY RUDGE, Cecil Hepworth, GB 1915
Tom Powers as Barnaby

directors like Christy Cabanne, Allan Dwan, Jack Conway, John Emerson, Edward Dillon and Paul Powell. Among the films he supervised were the early comedies of Douglas Fairbanks.

In March, 1917, Griffith sailed for England, where he was received like and by Royalty. He made an official tour of the Western Front with his cameraman, Billy Bitzer, and he soon conceived the idea of a film showing the horrors of war and the atrocities of the Germans. He wrote his script, got his players from America and made many trips from England to France, where he photographed hundreds of thousands of feet of film on the battlefields. A great deal of this material passed into government archives, but he also used it as background material for several of his films, principally *Hearts of the World* which had its New York première on 4th April 1918, in an atmosphere of war fever.

The Triangle Company, which consisted of Griffith, Mack Sennett and Thomas Ince, was a grouping of the three greatest talents in America. Thomas Ince began his film career as an actor with Biograph. Then for Bison 101 he made Westerns such as *Across the Plains* and *The Deserter*, both in 1912. In 1913 began his collaboration with the distinguished script writer C. Gardner

THE VAMPIRES, Louis Feuillade, France 1915

Sullivan. Unlike Griffith, Ince had an ordered approach to films. Everything was on paper, everything was organised. In this way it became easier for him to supervise many films, and his studio practice became very much a part of American film production. Among the directors whose work he guided were Reginald Barker, Lambert Hillyer, Francis Ford and Frank Borzage. Becoming Director General of the New York Motion Picture Company in California, he made a number of films such as *The Coward* (1915) with Charles Ray, a young actor whose *The Hired Man* (1918) and *The Old Swimming Hole* (1921) were to become very popular. The appearance of the remarkable Japanese actor Sessue Hayakawa and his wife Tsuru Aoki in *The Wrath of the Gods* and *Typhoon* in 1914 won the devotion of fans and represented a racial breakthrough into the Hollywood film, although in the past Red Indian actors like Red Feather had had their following. Ince's greatest star, however, was William S. Hart, whose Western films *Between Men* (1915), *The Fugitive* (1916), *The Aryan* (1916), and *Blue Blazes Rawdon* (1918) set a pattern for the genre. In *Civilisation* (1915) Ince undertook an ambitious subject on pacifism and told the

THE SONS OF INGMAR, Victor Sjöström, Sweden 1918
Victor Sjöström, Svenska

story of a man possessed by the spirit of Christ who tries to prevent war. The subject was controversial, as America was poised to enter the European conflict. The film lacks the driving force and imagination of Griffith, but it was considered outstanding in its day.

The Keystone series of Chaplin appeared in 1914 and it was clear that a new phenomenon had arrived. This perky little tramp, who had evolved from Sennett's slapstick comedies and who was in constant conflict with the forces of law and order, found his way into the hearts of millions. His brilliant miming, his use of pathos in the midst of hilarious fun and, above all, his humanity struck a sympathetic chord with people all over the world. Even today such films as *Dough and Dynamite, His Trysting Place, Tillie's Punctured Romance* (with Marie Dressler) make audiences rock with laughter. His first leading lady, Mabel Normand, also did much to contribute to his success, in films like *Mabel's Busy Day, Mabel at the Wheel* and *Mabel's Strange Predicament.* In 1915 Chaplin moved to Essanay where he further developed the character of the little tramp in films like *A Night Out, The Champion, Shanghaied* and *Carmen.* His leading lady was now Edna Purviance, who also continued with him in the series he made for Mutual in 1916–17. These included *Easy Street,* which well may be his masterpiece. In 1918 he moved to First National Films and in that year made *A Dog's Life, The Bond* and *Shoulder Arms.*

Mary Pickford, the curly-headed little Mary of Biograph days, had come a long way in the affections of audiences. Her mischievous vitality and charm, her aggressiveness in defence of the underdog and her epitomisation of all the old moral virtues, gave her added strength. She was a shrewd business woman and saw to it that she maintained high technical standards in her films. Maurice Tourneur directed her in two films, *Poor Little Rich Girl* (1917) and *Pride of the Clan* (1917). Marshall Neilan directed *The Little Princess* (1917), *M'Liss* (1918) and *Stella Maris* (1918). Other pictures of hers included *Rebecca of Sunnybrook Farm* (1917) and *Tess of the Storm Country* (1914), as well as a very delightful *Madame Butterfly* directed by Sidney Olcott in 1915, in which Marshall Neilan was her leading man.

American directors were developing rapidly. *The Cheat* (1915) by Cecil B. de Mille and featuring Fanny Ward and Sessue Hayakawa attracted much attention, particularly in France, for its refinement of technique and lighting. Its story of intrigue in high levels of society suited the mood of the time. In the same year de Mille made *Carmen* with Geraldine Farrar and Wallace Reid, and he

THE PRIDE OF THE CLAN, Maurice Tourneur, USA 1917
Mary Pickford

used the same pair in *Joan the Woman* (1917), exploiting his flair for spectacle. His *Whispering Chorus* (1918) used the theme of duty to one's country.

In 1916 Rex Ingram, a young Irishman who graduated from writing scripts for Theda Bara and Betty Nansen at Fox and acting with Edison and Vitagraph, directed his own story *The Great Problem* for Universal. He was then twenty-three years old. Two of his most important films of this period were *Black Orchids* and *Chalice of Sorrow*, both starring Cleo Madison, an actress of exceptional talent and beauty. The latter film was an adaptation of *La Tosca* set in Mexican surroundings. Ingram's films were noted for their fine pictorial qualities and romanticism.

Other early directors of distinction include J. Searle Dawley who worked with Edison, George Baker who worked with J. Stuart Blackton at Vitagraph, and the Irishman Herbert Brenon, who directed the Annette Kellerman spectacles, *Neptune's Daughter* (1914) and *A Daughter of the Gods* (1916). Annette Kellerman was a swimming specialist of her day and this gave her the opportunity of revealing more of her charms than her rivals. Brenon also made the important *War Brides* (1916), thus introducing the sensational Nazimova and Richard Barthlemess to the screen. Another director, J. Gordon Edwards, was mainly notable for the direction of Theda Bara films. This star was the prototype of all vamps. She began her career in *A Fool There Was* directed by Frank Powell in 1915. Then followed a whole gallery of destructive females—*Carmen* (1915), *Salome* (1918), *Cleopatra* (1917), *Dubarry* (1917) and *Camille* (1917).

The French director Maurice Tourneur brought to his American films a rich pictorial sense, a wide range of subjects and an

THE PAWN OF FATE
Maurice Tourneur directs Frank Keenan, 1916

Tom Mix, popular cowboy star of the twenties

ability to handle players. His most outstanding films of this period include *The Wishing Ring* (1914), *Alias Jimmy Valentine* (1915), *Trilby* (1916) and *The Bluebird* (1918).

Erich von Stroheim made his first film, *Blind Husbands*, in 1917. In it he indicated the future style of his films and their sophisticated and often cynical approach to intimate human problems. He created the role of the ruthless and selfish seducer in this story of a mountain guide who comes between a husband and wife.

The serial films thrived. *The Exploits of Elaine* and *The Perils of Pauline*, with the popular Pearl White, had set a fashion. Helen Holmes with her railway dramas and Ruth Roland with her rough-riding followed suit. Audiences loved the suspense as each week their favourites did their cliff-hanging or got trapped by wild beasts. The dangers of land, sea and air were fully exploited.

In France Feuillade was still working at his métier. *Les Vampires* appeared in 1915, *Judex* in 1916 and *The New Mission of Judex* in 1918. A new wave of directors was maturing. Antoine of the Théâtre Libre turned his attention to the cinema. His theories of naturalism were put to the test and he started off with *The Corsican*

Brothers (1916). Hugo's *Toilers of the Sea* was made in 1918. He tried to keep his settings true to the environment of the story and controlled his players to convey the impression of real life.

Less concerned with reality was Abel Gance, who was born in Paris on 28th October 1889. After an unpromising start in the theatre Gance directed some Pathé costume dramas. Then came *The Mask of Horror* with de Max. *The Madness of Dr Tube* (1915) was distinguished for its use of distorted sets. 1916 saw his serial *Barberousse* and *The Zone of Death*, the latter dealing with destruction on a cosmic scale. His *Mater Dolorosa* of the following year was a dramatic triangle story told with rich imagery and fine photography by Burel. In 1918 came *The Tenth Symphony*. It was a characteristic Gance effort. His inability to see the wood from the trees in his ambitious landscapes, and his overblown poetic effects, mar the personal and imaginative quality of his films. He tried very hard, but he lacked the discipline and judgement of a truly great director.

An important development in France was the appearance of the first great film critic, Louis Delluc, who was born at Cadouin in the Dordogne district in 1890. His family moved to Paris where he became passionately interested in the theatre, had several plays produced and wrote theatre criticism. Converted to films by his wife, Eve Francis, the actress, he became equally enthusiastic on this subject, and he came out strongly in favour of films which advanced the art of the cinema.

The work of Sjöström and Stiller continued in Sweden. *Terje Vigen* (1916) by Sjöström was based on a poem by Ibsen, which told of a Norwegian arrested for trying to break a blockade of a village by British ships and bring grain to the starving people. It was filmed like a documentary and had an impressive scene where the hero, Terje Vigen, is chased in his rowing boat by British soldiers. Its landscapes and seascapes create the mood and feeling of the film. *The Outlaw and His Wife* (1918) was a story of Iceland taken from a theatrical piece. It tells of the love of Berg Eyvind for a widow farmer and of the enmity they excite in a jealous bailiff. They are forced to take to the hills where, for a time, life is happy, but eventually they are driven to the higher slopes where they perish in the snow. Sjöström's feeling for nature was never so well expressed as in this film. He himself played the hero, while the woman was played by his wife, Edith Erastoff.

Mauritz Stiller was best known for his *Madame de Thebes* (1915)

THE CHEAT, Cecil B. de Mille, USA 1915 ▶
Sessue Hayakawa and Fanny Ward, Paramount

FATHER SERGIUS, Protozanov, USSR 1918
Ivan Mosjoukine

and *Anjuta the Dancer* (1916) before he made his masterpiece, *Song of the Red Flower* (1918). This was a story of lumbermen and their romantic rivalries. The leading role was taken by Lars Hanson who was to feature in so many Swedish film classics. A new talent from the Skandia Company appeared in John Brunius, whose charming tales of rural Sweden were exemplified by *Puss in Boots* (1918).

In Russia the Czarist cinema was well established and popular. Its themes were sensational, violent and morbid but it developed directors of importance, such as Drankov, Goncharov and Protozanov. Starevitch broke new ground with his puppet films. Eugene Bauer was a director of special distinction who influenced Ivan Mosjoukine, the great romantic player of his time. The following films deserve mention: *The Portrait of Dorian Gray* (1915) by Meyerhold; *A Life for a Life* (1916) and *The Revolutionist* (1917) by Bauer; *The Queen of Spades* (1916), *Andre Kozhukov* (1917) and *Father Sergius* (1918) by Protozanov. With the coming of the Revolution, the pattern of Russian films changed and a number of the old guard fled to Europe via the Crimea. The greater number settled in France and these included Volkoff, Tourjanski, Protozanov, Mosjoukine, Nathalie Lissenko and Nicolai Koline, as well as studio technicians and cameramen.

Italy continued with its spectacles. Guazzoni contributed *Jerusalem Delivered* and *Fabiola* in 1917, and a popular *Madame Tallien* (1915) with the beautiful Lyda Borelli. Emilio Ghione made *The Grey Rats* as Italy's contribution to the serial vogue of 1918. Eleanora Duse appeared in *Ashes* (1916) by Febo Mari. Pastrone made two less spectacular films, *The Fire* (1915) and *Royal Tigress* (1917). Gustavo Serena's *Assunta Spina* (1915) starred Francesca Bertini in a realistic drama of lower middle-class life.

Great Britain turned out a number of patriotic films. There was a tendency, too, to film all the popular novelists of the day—Marie Corelli, Rita, Hall Caine, as well as the dramatists Wilde, Pinero and Robertson. Increasingly famous stage figures like H. B. Irving, Ellen Terry, Sir John Hare and Sir George Alexander honoured the films in, respectively, *The Lyons Mail* (1917), *Her Greatest Performance* (1917), *Caste* (1916), *The Second Mrs Tanqueray* (1916). The Hepworth Company made *The Chimes* (1914), *Sweet Lavender* (1915), *Barnaby Rudge* (1915), *Comin' Thro' the Rye* (1916), *The American Heiress* (1917) and *The Bottle* (1915) with Albert Chevalier. Will Barker produced an ambitious *Jane Shore* (1915) and a version of Conan Doyle's *Brigadier Gerard* (1915). In the following year he made a version of Rider Haggard's *She* with Alice Delysia, and a melodrama, *Trapped by London Sharks.* Maurice Elvey, just beginning to make his name as a director, undertook *Dombey and Son* (1918). George Pearson, soon to be a considerable name in British films, made the Ultus series in 1916–17 as well as *The Better' Ole* (1918). Larry Trimble and his star Florence Turner came from Vitagraph to form Turner Films, for which they made *My Old Dutch* (1915) with Albert Chevalier, *Alone in London* (1915) and a version of Thomas Hardy's *Far From the Madding Crowd* (1916). Another American, George Loane Tucker, directed Henry Ainley in *The Prisoner of Zenda* and *Rupert of Hentzau* (both 1915). For Broadwest, E. Hay Plumb directed Ronald Colman in *A Son of David* (1918).

Germany provided Paul Wegener's *Rubezahl's Wedding* (1916) and *The Rat Catcher of Hamelin* (1917), and Otto Rippert's *Homunculus* (1916), the ancestor of the screen's mechanical men right down to Frankenstein.

With the end of the war the pattern of the cinema changed. The dominating force was now the Hollywood film. It was well organised and publicised, it had a striking array of popular stars, its style was fast-moving and exciting and it was nothing if not up-to-date. After the horrors and tragedy of war a reaction set in : the Gay Twenties had arrived. In Hollywood everything was larger than life. Conventions were overthrown. Occasional scandals from the movie capital hinted at exotic sin, and there is nothing that the middle classes love more. The cinema enjoyed its greatest popularity during these years and fan magazines catered for every aspect of their readers' curiosity.

If any one movement influenced the cinema strongly after the First World War, it was the German cinema. The defeat of the Germans brought in its wake disorder and chaos, revolution, poverty and hunger. The new movement of Expressionism and other artistic strivings became focused on the cinema. Deriving from the standards set by the great theatre of Max Reinhardt, actors, designers, painters and architects flocked to the studios. Brilliant cameramen like Fritz Arno Wagner, Carl Hoffman, Guido Seeber and many others had come to realise the functional purpose of the camera in relation to the grand design of the director. The chief merit of the German film was its perfect co-ordination of the various elements which go to make up a film : the story, the setting, the acting and the unifying sequence of images.

1919 was a remarkable year all over the film world. Ernst Lubitsch, with his *Madame Dubarry* (1919), made perhaps the most marked impression. He had begun his artistic career with Reinhardt and then became a film comedian. The polish and sophistication he brought to his historical subjects, his flair for the handling of crowds and his tasteful mounting of the films marked him out as a master of his medium. His *Sumurun* and *Anna Boleyn* (1920) and *The Loves of Pharaoh* (1922) consolidated his position as a great film-maker. He used the best actors available, such as Emil Jannings, Pola Negri, Paul Wegener and Henny Porten, and his German films were all photographed by Theodor Sparkuhl. In 1923 he went to America to direct Mary Pickford's *Rosita*, and his subsequent career lay there.

MADAME DUBARRY, Ernst Lubitsch, Germany 1919
Emil Jannings and Pola Negri

57

The most revolutionary film from Germany was, however, *The Cabinet of Dr Caligari* by Dr Robert Wiene. This story of a madman's fantasy was presented in a setting of tortured streets and rooms designed in a cubist style. Its players, Werner Krauss, Conrad Veidt and Lil Dagover, carried this feeling into their playing. There has never been a film quite like this and its influence has been felt all through the cinema. The settings were by Herman Warm and the story was by Carl Mayer, a man who was to be responsible for so much that was valuable in the German cinema. Wiene made another film with fantastic settings, *Genuine*, also scripted by Mayer, and a more conventional *Der Rosenkavalier* (1926) with the French stars Huguette Duflos and Jacques Catelain.

Fritz Lang, the son of a Viennese architect, studied painting and architecture before the war. Wounded while in action, he began writing scenarios, then drifted into the direction of his stories which were mostly sensational adventure and crime films, such as

THE CABINET OF DR CALIGARI, Robert Wiene, Germany 1919 Conrad Veidt, Decla Bioscop

THE CABINET OF DR CALIGARI, Robert Wiene, Germany 1919
Design by Herman Warm, Decla Bioscop

the two-part *The Spiders* (1919). Previously he had written the scripts for Otto Rippert's *Plague in Florence* (1919) and later for Joe May's *The Indian Tomb* (1920). In 1921 he directed the beautiful *The Tired Death*, which tells of a woman granted three lives to enable her to save one for which, in return, she can have her lover back from death. She fails but is reunited with her lover in death. The scenes are set in ancient Baghdad, ancient China and 17th-century Venice. The beauty of Warm's settings and the camera-work of Fritz Arno Wagner unite with Lang's pictorial sense to make a memorable film. The script was the combined work of Lang and his wife, Thea von Harbou, one of the most talented script-writers in Germany, who worked with Lang on all his German films. In 1922 came the two-part film *Dr Mabuse*, based on a novel by Norbert Jacques. This was very much in the Feuillade tradition. A mysterious criminal, famous for his disguises and his capacity for penetrating all ranks of society, is eventually brought to heel by a police official. In spite of its exaggerated situations it reflects the mood prevailing in the Berlin of its time. Rudolph Klein-Rogge as Mabuse and Bernhardt Goetzke as his opponent gave fine performances in a film which was regarded as sensational then and which still has the power to grip one's attention.

In 1923–24 Lang was engaged in the making of his epic *The Nibelungs*, in two parts, *Siegfried* and *Kriemhild's Revenge*. Breath-taking in its architectural scale, it used Lang's pictorial eye to good effect. It has been criticised for its static and formal

THE TIRED DEATH, Fritz Lang, Germany 1921
Death in Venice, Decla Bioscop

KRIEMHILD'S REVENGE, Fritz Lang, Germany 1923–24
Margarethe Schoen and Bernhardt Goetzke, Decla Bioscop

SIEGFRIED, Fritz Lang, Germany 1923–24
Paul Richter as Siegfried bathes in the dragon's blood, Decla
Bioscop

qualities but this, to my mind, is a mistake. The real dramatic conflict in the film is between Part One and Part Two. In the first, the formal beauty of Siegfried's world and the slow delicate winning of Kriemhild's love make for a static pattern. But when Siegfried is treacherously murdered, the hatred of Kriemhild is unleashed. Gone are the beautiful forests and the architectural dignity of the castles, and we have the monstrous Attila to replace the image of Siegfried, the barbaric décors to take the place of the sets of Gunthur's court. The end of the film is a swift-moving holocaust of destructive action.

METROPOLIS, Fritz Lang, Germany 1926
Birth of a Robot, Brigitte Helm, UFA

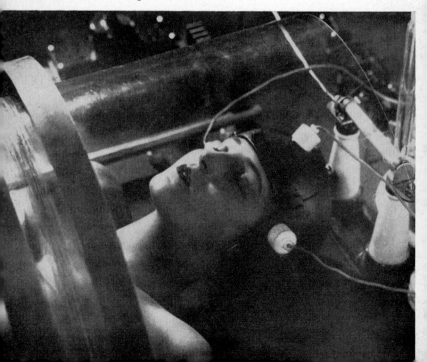

Lang made three more silent films. *Metropolis* (1926), a prophecy of the future fate of mankind, *Spies* (1928), a return to a Mabuse subject, and *The Girl in the Moon* (1928), a science-fiction film. In the first of these the settings were breath-taking. The architecture of the city of the future, the birth of the robot, the flooding of the workers' quarters and the explosion of the machines were unforgettable. In the last film the departure of the rocket for the moon more than compensated for a weak human story. In these films Lang introduced two new actresses—the beautiful Brigitte Helm in *Metropolis* and Gerda Maurus in the other two.

METROPOLIS, Fritz Lang, Germany 1926
The City of the Future. UFA

SPIES, Fritz Lang, Germany 1928
Paul Hörbiger, Gerda Maurus and Rudolph Klein-Rogge, UFA

Ewald André Dupont made two main contributions to the German cinema. His story of an ambitious young Jew who breaks with his family tradition and becomes an actor in Vienna's famous Burg Theater, was directed with a fine sense of atmosphere and a much more open-air quality than was characteristic of German films. This film, *The Ancient Law* (1923), had Ernst Deutsch and Henny Porten in its cast. But Dupont will always be remembered by his masterpiece, *Vaudeville* (1925), a truly virtuoso film of love and jealousy among variety performers. Its camera-work by Karl Freund, its settings by Oscar Werndorff and its fine playing by Emil Jannings, Lya de Putti and Warwick Ward made it almost a perfect film.

VAUDEVILLE, E. A. Dupont, Germany 1925
Lya de Putti and Emil Jannings, UFA

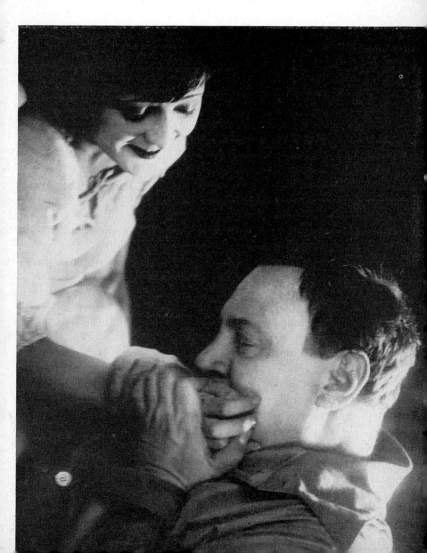

The career of Arthur von Gerlach is unusual. He originally came to films from the theatre. Before his death in 1926 he made only two films, both of the highest merit. *Vanina* (1922) was based on the Stendhal tale of a tyrant. It had a powerful combination of players, Paul Wegener, Asta Nielsen and Paul Hartmann. Its intense style was almost expressionist and the talent of its director was obvious. His next film was *The Chronicles of the Grey House* (1923), based on a novel by Theodore Storm. Here the mood was one of the open air and the wind on the heath. A feud between brothers over an inheritance, the brooding spirit of the old house, the passing of time, these were the elements of the film. Thea von Harbou wrote the script, Fritz Arno Wagner photographed, and the settings of Röhrig and Herlth carried the ingenuity of the German designer on to the heath itself.

THE CHRONICLES OF THE GREY HOUSE ▶
Arthur von Gerlach, Germany 1923, On Luneberg Heath, UFA

VANINA, Arthur von Gerlach, Germany 1922
Paul Wegener and Asta Nielsen

THE LAST LAUGH, F. W. Murnau, Germany 1924
Emil Jannings, UFA

TARTUFFE, F. W. Murnau, Germany 1925
Emil Jannings, UFA

Another director who seemed able to maintain contact with the world of nature was F. W. Murnau, perhaps the greatest German film-maker. He was born in Bielefeld, Westphalia, in 1889. Theatrical experience with Reinhardt, interrupted by war, led him to films. Of his earlier films the most important are: *Janus Faced* (1920), a variation of the Jekyll and Hyde theme which featured Conrad Veidt; *The Haunted Castle* (1921) with Paul Hartmann and Olga Tschechowa, which was noted for its atmospheric and impressionist sets; *The Burning Acre* (1922), a story of peasant life with Werner Krauss, Eugen Klöpfer and Lya de Putti; *Nosferatu* (1922), a pirated version of *Dracula* handled with fine sense of atmosphere and doom, and *Phantom* (1922), a story by Gerhardt Hauptmann which tells of a man dragged to degradation by his daydreams. With *The Last Laugh* (1924), Murnau reached the height of his achievement. This story by Carl Mayer tells of an old hotel commissionaire, too enfeebled to carry out his duties, who is demoted to lavatory attendant. No titles were used. The camera of Karl Freund told the story. Emil Jannings, only twenty-nine at the time, gave his greatest performance as the old man, and the settings of Röhrig and Herlth provided expressive background for the action. This film is a masterpiece. *Tartuffe* (1925), made with the same team, is more a triumph for Jannings than for Murnau.

69

To see his next picture, *Faust* (1926), is to plunge into a medieval existence. Murnau lays the world of Breughel, Hieronymus Bosch and Dürer before us. The beauty of the scenes is overwhelming. Faust is played by the Swedish actor Gösta Ekman, Camilla Horn is Marguerite, Yvette Guilbert is Martha and Jannings as Mephisto brings a robust and slyly humorous quality to his Devil. The outcome of this striking career was that Murnau was invited to America to film Sudermann's *A Trip to Tilsit*.

G. W. Pabst, with his intense interest in the psychology of his characters, was to take the German film into new territory. Man in the social scene interested him and although he began with films

FAUST, F. W. Murnau, Germany 1926
Gösta Ekman, UFA

GÖSTA BERLING SAGA, Mauritz Stiller, Sweden 1923
Greta Garbo and Tors Hammeren, Svenska

of a conventional nature, his *Joyless Street* (1925) showed his special merits. This sordid story of the inflationary period with its hunger and degradation is vividly brought to life. Greta Garbo, fresh from her success in *Gösta Berling Saga*, played the sensitive virtuous girl forced by circumstances to work in a brothel, and Asta Nielsen as a tragic figure of the demi-monde, Werner Krauss as the gross butcher who had the working people at his mercy and Valeska Gert as the Madame, gave the performances of their career. Pabst invested the scene where the people queue for food with a pitiable urgency.

SECRETS OF THE SOUL, G. W. Pabst, Germany 1926
Werner Krauss and Ilke Gruening, UFA

Secrets of the Soul (1926), in which Werner Krauss played the
lead, was a serious treatment of psycho-analysis. *The Love of
Jeanne Ney* (1927) dealt with modern lives caught up in the net
of Revolution and was based on a novel by Ilya Ehrenburg. Again
Pabst's character drawing is flawless, as are the settings he creates
for his action. Brigitte Helm, Edith Jehanne, Fritz Rasp and Uno
Henning give fine performances. *Crisis* (1928) was a study of a
neurotic woman played by Brigitte Helm. In the American actress
Louise Brooks, Pabst found a suitable interpreter of his *Pandora's
Box* (1928), based on two plays of Wedekind. This powerful
study of a woman incapable of foreseeing the consequence of her
actions, who destroys everything she touches and in the end is
destroyed by the forces she sets in motion, is handled with a
masterly touch by Pabst. He again used Miss Brooks in *Diary of
a Lost Girl* (1929). For both films he had the invaluable services of
Ernö Metzner as designer.

THE STUDENT OF PRAGUE,
Henrik Galeen, Germany 1926, Conrad Veidt

PANDORA'S BOX, G. W. Pabst, Germany 1928
Lulu and Jack the Ripper

The great richness of the German cinema makes it almost impossible to do justice to the many films of considerable merit produced: *Algol* (1920) by Hans Werkmeister with Jannings and most effective sets; *From Morn To Midnight* (1920), another expressionist experiment by Karl Heinz Martin; *The Golem* (1920), *The Student of Prague* (1926) and *Alraune* (1928) by Henrik Galeen, outstanding examples of studio-craftsmanship; the street films, *The Street* (1923) by Karl Grüne, *Small Town Sinners* (1927) and *Tragedy of the Street* (1927) by Bruno Rahn, and the films of Lupu Pick, *Rails* (1921), *Sylvestre* (1923) and *The Wild Duck* (1925). The decorative film is best represented by *Waxworks* (1924) by Paul Leni and *Warning Shadows* (1923) by Arthur Robison.

ALGOL, Hans Werkmeister, Germany 1920
Setting by Walther Reimann

WAXWORKS, Paul Leni, Germany 1924
Conrad Veidt as Ivan the Terrible

THE GOLEM, Henrik Galeen, Germany 1920 ▶
Revolt in the Ghetto

THE GOLEM, Henrik Galeen, Germany 1920
Paul Wegener

SECRETS OF THE EAST, Alexander Volkoff, Germany 1928
The Sultan's Palace, UFA

LADY HAMILTON, Richard Oswald, Germany 1921
Conrad Veidt and Liane Haid

The costume and spectacle film formed a large part of the German product and one should mention *Danton* (1920), *Othello* (1922), *Peter the Great* (1923), all by Dmitri Buchowetzski; *Monna Vanna* (1922) by Richard Eichberg; *Lucretia Borgia* (1922), *Lady Hamilton* (1921) and *Carlos and Elizabeth* (1924), by Richard Oswald, and *Nathan the Wise* (1923) and *The Fall of Troy* (1924), both by Manfred Noa.

Other directors worth mention are Dr Ludwig Berger for his *Cinderella* (1923) and *A Glass of Water* (1923), which exploited Baroque design; Karl Grüne for his *Jealousy* (1926), *The Brothers Schellenberg* (1926) and *At the Edge of the World* (1927); Dr Paul Czinner for his direction of the Elizabeth Bergner films, *Nju* (1924), *Violinist of Florence* (1926), *Liebe* (1927), *Donna Juana* (1928) and *Fraulein Else* (1929); and Arnold Fanck for his wonderful mountain films, *Peak of Destiny* (1924), *The Sacred Mountain*, *The Big Jump* (1927) and *The White Hell of Pitz Palu* (1929). In the last three films Fanck starred the distinguished

81

dancer and mountain climber, Leni Riefenstahl, and in the last film he had the co-operation of G. W. Pabst.

Finally the experimental work of men like Viking Eggeling, Hans Richter, Fischinger, Ernö Metzner and Walter Ruttman should not be forgotten. Also noteworthy were Piel Jutzi's proletarian drama *Mother Krausen* (1930) and *People on Sunday* (1929), made by a formidable group consisting of Robert Siodmak, Edgar Ulmer, Billy Wilder and Fred Zinnemann, all of whom were to play big parts in American films.

CARLOS AND ELIZABETH, Richard Oswald, Germany 1924
Conrad Veidt as Don Carlos

SIR ARNE'S TREASURE, Mauritz Stiller, Sweden 1919
Richard Lund and Mary Johnson
Sir Archy uses Elsalill as a shield. Svenska

In spite of the strong competition from America, the Scandinavian
countries continued to make their contribution to the cinema in
the twenties. Stiller's *Sir Arne's Treasure* (1919), based on
Selma Lagerlöf's novel, is steeped in an atmosphere of snowy
winter and primitive hates and passions. The very different
Erotikon (1920) is a sophisticated comedy of modern life which

THE EMIGRANTS, Mauritz Stiller, Sweden 1921
Lars Hanson and Jenny Hasselquist, Svenska

anticipates the work of Lubitsch. There followed *Johan* (1920), *The Emigrants* (1921), *Gunnar Hedes Saga* (1922) and the ambitious *Gösta Berling Saga* (1923). The latter was based on Lagerlöf's most famous novel and launched Greta Garbo on her career. It was a long, complex film and had three heroines, played by Mona Martenson, Jenny Hasselquist and Garbo. The title role was played by Lars Hanson. The most outstanding performance was that given by Gerda Lundequist in her unforgettable role of the Mistress of Ekeby. This was the end of Stiller's work in Sweden. He went to Hollywood with his new star, but success eluded him and he returned to die in Sweden in 1928.

Sjöström launched his *Secret of the Monastery* (1919), from a story by Grillparzer, and *Karin Ingmarsdotter* (1919), a section of Lagerlöf's *Jerusalem,* a book which was to inspire no less than five films. In *Karen Ingmarsdotter* the great Tore Teja portrayed a peasant girl in vivid contrast to her sophisticated modern woman in *Erotikon*; the Swedes had the advantage of brilliant players and Garbo was by no means the best of them. With *The Phantom Coach* (1920) Sjöström became a world success. This limited story got bravura treatment and carried the art of film story-telling to new levels. Sjöström's last important film in Sweden, *Love's Crucible* (1921), was a medieval story of great pictorial beauty. It has been compared with Eisenstein's work and tells of a woman's ordeal in a trial by fire. Jenny Hasselquist gave an outstanding performance.

Other Swedish directors of this time were: John Brunius—*The Gay Knight* (1920), *A Norway Lass* (1920), *The Burning Mill* (1921), *Johan Ulfstierna* (1923) and *Charles XII* (1924); Ivan Hedquist—*In Search of Happiness* (1919); Gustav Molander—*Pirates of Lake Mälar* (1923), *Jerusalem* (1926). Sweden can also claim *The Witch* (1920) by the Danish director Benjamin Christensen, a grisly and almost documentary treatment of witchcraft in medieval times linked with an epilogue on modern superstitions and neuroses. It was a daring film in both subject and treatment.

LOVE'S CRUCIBLE, Victor Sjöström, Sweden 1921
The Trial by Fire. Svenska

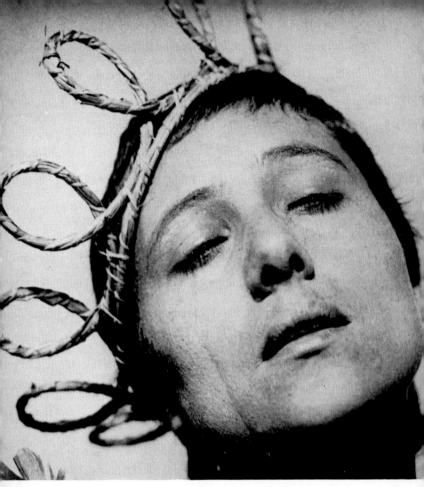

THE PASSION OF JOAN OF ARC, Carl Dreyer, France 1928
Falconetti

In Carl Dreyer, Denmark gave the world a major figure of the cinema. His first film, *The President*, was made in 1919. In the following year came *Leaves from Satan's Book* (1920), depicting the death of Christ, the Spanish Inquisition, the French Revolution and Communism in modern Finland. His charming *The Minister's Wife* (1920) is told with sympathy and humour and concerns a newly appointed clergyman who, according to custom, must marry the relict of his predecessor. *Master of the House* (1925), a delightful domestic comedy, was handled with Dreyer's usual uncompromising insight into his characters, a quality he used to most effect in his *tour de force*, *The Passion of Joan of Arc,* made in France in 1928. With this film Dreyer achieved one of the most original works ever seen on the screen. His concentrated exploration of his actress Falconetti produced results which were almost painful to watch. The design by Herman Warm helped to suggest the period and at the same time to focus attention on the main characters. Other Danish films, such as the Dickens films of A. W. Sandberg, *Our Mutual Friend* (1919), *Great Expectations* (1921), *David Copperfield* (1922), and *Little Dorrit* (1924), and *The Clown* (1926) won fame abroad; but the day of Denmark's film greatness was over and her players and directors drifted into the German film industry.

MASTER OF THE HOUSE, Carl Dreyer, Denmark 1925
Mathilde Nielsen and Johannes Meyer

France, too, had lost her film supremacy after the war, but with her usual intellectual drive she made up in quality what she lacked in quantity. She had her eclectic, daring spirits but her commercial products also showed a high sense of craftsmanship.

Abel Gance was perhaps the most flamboyant director of his time. His themes were large, very often unmanageable, but full of inventiveness and technical bravura. *J'Accuse* (1919), in which the war dead came back to accuse the living, was a strong indictment of war, and *The Wheel* (1922) a mixture of symbolic imagery wasted on a melodramatic plot about a blinded engine-driver. His most ambitious film, *Napoleon* (1927), was planned for multiple projectors on a triple screen. In magnificence, inventiveness and obsessional hero-worship it is unique.

In 1921 Jacques Feyder produced *Woman of Atlantis* with the rather portly Napierkowska in the role of Antinea. The exotic settings and desert atmosphere made a considerable impact. Feyder's next films, *Crainquebille* (1922) and *Visages d'Enfants*

THERESE RAQUIN, Jacques Feyder, France 1929 ▶
Return from Murder

NAPOLEON, Abel Gance, France 1926
Roudenko

90

(1924), were on a simpler scale and featured the sensitive child-actor Jean Forest who shared honours in the former with the veteran, Maurice de Feraudy. Feyder made *The Image* (1926) in Austria, *Carmen* (1926) in Spain with Raquel Meller, and a powerful *Thérèse Raquin* (1929) in Germany with Gina Manes and Jeanne Marie Laurent. Before leaving for Hollywood he made the controversial satire *The New Gentlemen* (1929).

Léon Poirier's films were noted for their freshness of ideas, their feeling for landscape and their concern for exotic backgrounds. *The Thinker* (1920) represented people's thoughts by much superimposition of images. *Jocelyn* (1922) and *La Brière* (1924) were noted for their exteriors and beautiful period flavour. *The Black Crusader* (1925) was a documentary of Africa and *Verdun* (1928) a fictional reconstruction of a war event.

The critic Louis Delluc directed *The Way to Ernoa* (1920) with a Basque setting. Then followed *Black Smoke* (1921), a detective story, and *The Silence* (1921), about a husband who has killed his wife and tells her story in remembered images. In this Eve

THE FLOOD, Louis Delluc, France 1923
Philippe Heriat, Ginette Maddie and Eve Francis

Francis, Delluc's wife and star of his films, gave a powerful performance. In *Fièvre* (1921) we are given a slice of life heavy with sadness and disillusion. In a sleazy dock-side bar people come and go, their lives intertwine, life explodes into violence and then resumes its mask. This was Delluc's greatest film. In 1922 memory was again the theme in *The Woman from Nowhere*, the study of an elderly woman who returns to the scene of a former romance and sees her story about to be re-enacted by a younger woman. His last film, *The Flood* (1923), derived from the Swedes. His early death at the age of thirty-three robbed the French cinema of one of its greatest talents.

The element of experiment owed much to the stimulus of Delluc. Germaine Dulac, who made solid commercial films like *The Death of the Sun* (1921) and *Soul of an Artist* (1925), produced *The Smiling Madame Beudet* (1923) and *The Seashell and the Clergyman* (1926). Dmitri Kirsanoff's *Menilmontant* (1924), with its poignant performance by Nadia Sibirskaia, Fernand Léger's *Mechanical Ballet* (1924), *Oddities* (1923) by Aut-

THE WATER GIRL, Jean Renoir, France 1924
Renoir's first film

ant-Lara, *Starfish* (1928) by Man Ray and *Concerning Nice* (1929) by Jean Vigo are typical of the experiments which went on in different quarters of French films. Jean Gremillon was another talented director who began with experimental films and later produced the two silent films for which he is known: *Maldone* (1928) and *Keepers of the Lighthouse* (1929).

Marcel l'Herbier, a poet, began his contact with films in the army film service. From scenarist he became director of *Man of the Deep* (1920), *El Dorado* (1922), *Don Juan and Faust* (1922), *The Inhuman One* (1923), *The Late Matthew Pascal* (1925), *Vertigo* (1927) and *Money* (1928). His films were literary in quality, drawing on Balzac, Zola and Pirandello. They were also notable, however, for their visual experiments and were practically a school for designers like Léger, Mallet-Stevens, Autant-Lara and Cavalcanti. His players, too, ranged from Eve Francis, Marcelle Pradot, Brigitte Helm, Jacques Catelain, Philip Heriat and Ivan Mosjoukine to Lois Moran (on whom Scott Fitzgerald based the heroine of *Tender is the Night*) and Georgette Leblanc, wife of Maeterlinck.

René Clair, a young actor in serials, began as an experimentalist in *The Crazy Ray* and *Entracte* (1924). With *The Italian Straw Hat* (1927), with its satiric picture of late-19th-century mores, he came into his own special brand of comedy, which he followed by *Two Timid Souls* (1928), portraying a difficult courtship.

Jean Epstein was a recruit from the world of literature. His *The Faithful Heart* (1923) was marked by camera virtuosity in its fairground scenes and a realistic approach to life. *La Belle Nivernaise* (1923) concentrated on landscape. After a number of more commercial films, Epstein became more personal with *The Fall of the House of Usher* (1928) and the documentary-like *End of the World* (1928), set on the Breton island of Ushant.

Antoine developed his naturalist style in *Mlle. de Seiglière* (1919) and *The Earth* (1921) by Zola, as well as in Daudet's *The Woman of Arles* (1922).

Luis Bunuel collaborated with Dali in the surrealist film *The Andalusian Dog* (1929), and Julien Duvivier made *The Miracle of Lourdes* (1924). Both were to make their major contributions in the period of the sound film.

◄ THE INHUMAN ONE, Marcel l'Herbier, France 1923
Set by Fernand Léger

Jean Renoir, son of the painter, directed *The Water Girl* (1924) and *Nana* (1926), in both of which his wife, Catherine Hessling, played. She also appeared in his more off-beat *Charleston* (1928) and *The Little Match Girl* (1929).

Alberto Cavalcanti, a Brazilian designer, made *Only the Hours* (1926), a film about the seamier side of city life, and *At Anchor* (1929), a dock-side drama with Delluc-like overtones. His experimental *La P'tite Lilie* (1927) and *Little Red Riding Hood* featured Catherine Hessling.

Jacques de Baroncelli is remembered for his literary transcriptions, *Father Goriot* (1922) by Balzac and *The Dream* (1923) by Zola, as well as for the sensitive atmospheres of *Nene* (1923) and *The Iceland Fishermen* (1922), with its Breton landscapes and fine performances by Charles Vanel and Sandra Milowanoff.

◀ THE LATE MATTHEW PASCAL, Marcel l'Herbier, France 1925
Marcelle Pradot and Ivan Mosjoukine

NANA, Jean Renoir, France 1926
Catherine Hessling and Valeska Gert

The big popular films of the French commercial cinema were not without merit. Bernard Deschamps' *Agony of the Eagles* (1921), Raymond Bernard's *Miracle of the Wolves* (1924) and *The Chess-player* (1927), both featuring Charles Dullin, Diamant—Berger's *Three Musketeers* (1921), Henry Roussell's *Imperial Violets* (1924) with Raquel Meller, Henri Fescourt's *Les Miserables* (1925), Léonce Perret's *Koenigsmark* (1924) and *Madame Sans Gêne* (1925) with Gloria Swanson, were some of the films which made the headlines.

The Russian *émigrés* settled down in the Montreuil district just outside Paris. Ivan Mosjoukine, one of the outstanding European actors, made a version of *Edmund Kean* (1924) which was directed by Alexander Volkoff, but over which Mosjoukine had considerable control. The editing of the tavern scenes with their riotous dancing anticipated later developments in Soviet editing, which makes one think that the use of montage may express basic

EDMUND KEAN, Alexander Volkoff, France 1924
Nicolai Koline and Ivan Mosjoukine

THE MIRACLE OF THE WOLVES, Raymond Bernard
France 1924

CASANOVA, Alexander Volkoff, France 1928
Ivan Mosjoukine, Suzanne Bianchetti

THE BURNING BRASIER, Ivan Mosjoukine, France 1923 ▶
Ivan Mosjoukine and Nathalie Lissenko

Russian attitudes. Mosjoukine himself directed *The Burning Brasier* (1923), a mixture of dreams and reality handled with a delicate humour and notable for the virtuoso multiple performances of Mosjoukine. He later played in Tourjanski's *Michael Strogoff* (1926) and the equally elaborate *Casanova* (1927) of Volkoff.

Italy's contribution to the cinema became less and less. Spectacles were still forthcoming, such as Guazzoni's *Messalina* (1923), Negroni's *Beatrice de Cenci* (1926) and *The Ship* (1920) by Gabriellino d'Annunzio, which told of Venice's early history and featured the dancer Ida Rubenstein. A German co-production of *Quo Vadis* (1925), directed by George Jacoby, featured Emil Jannings, while Carmine Gallone's *The Last Days of Pompeii* (1926) starred the international players Maria Korda, Bernhardt Goetzke and Victor Varconi. Other important films were Mario Bonnard's *The Betrothed* (1923) and Augusto Genina's *Cyrano de Bergerac* (1923), while at the very end of the silent period Blasetti's *The Sun* (1928) and Camerini's *Rails* (1929) seemed to usher in a more realistic approach.

The Czech cinema produced at least one outstanding director. Gustav Machaty's *From Saturday to Sunday* (1928) and *Erotikon* (1929) had individuality and style. His *Extase* (1931), though issued with a sound track, was conceived as a silent film.

There was much activity in Austria, where the Sascha Studios of Vienna gave Hungarian directors such as Michael Kertesz and Alexander Korda a chance to make spectacles such as *Sodom and Gomorrah* (1923), *Samson and Delilah* (1926) and *Moon of Israel* (1924). Holland produced an exceptionally brilliant documentary film-maker in Joris Ivens, whose *The Bridge* (1928) and *Rain* (1929) are well-observed essays on reality.

India, China and Japan were thriving film-producing countries, but their output never reached the western market, and almost nothing was known about Japan until a belated interest in her films of the fifties led to the discovery of a solid tradition of Japanese cinema. Certainly Teinosuke Kinugasa's full-blooded and powerful *Crossways* (1928) proves that the silent Japanese cinema was a highly sophisticated one. Kinugasa studied with Eisenstein, and his story of a man's flight from a crime he did not in fact commit was preceded by *A Crazy Page* (1927), which used impressionist techniques to depict life in a lunatic asylum.

The British film industry suffered many financial crises. The most prolific director was Maurice Elvey. His films include *Nelson* (1919) with Donald Calthrop, *The Fruitful Vine* (1921) with Valia and Basil Rathbone, *The Passionate Friends* (1922), based on the

BY THE LAW, Lev Kuleshov, USSR 1926 ▶
A story by Jack London

H. G. Wells novel, *Don Quixote* (1923) with Jerrold Robertshaw and George Robey, *The Wandering Jew* (1923), a spectacular film set in several ages, with Matheson Lang, *The Flag Lieutenant* (1926) with Henry Edwards and the war comedy *Mademoiselle From Armentières* (1926) with the charming Estelle Brody.

Adrian Brunel was an intelligent director but somehow did not find this an asset. His *Man Without Desire* (1923), with Ivor Novello and Ninna Vanna, relied on the idea of transmigration and settings in the style of Canaletto and Guardi. *Blighty* (1927) showed the reactions of a British upper class family to war, its players including Godfrey Winn, Lilian Hall-Davis and Nadia Sibirskaia. *The Constant Nymph* (1928), based on Margaret Kennedy's popular novel, had Ivor Novello and Mabel Poulton.

The pioneer Hepworth Company made *The Amazing Quest of Mr Edward Bliss* (1920) and finished their career with a remake of *Comin' Thro' the Rye* (1923). George Pearson, with the aid of the clever comedienne Betty Balfour, made the Squibs series, the first of which, *Squibs*, appeared in 1922. The Pearson films showed a real sense of craftsmanship. The Broadwest Company's most popular film was *Kissing Cup's Race* (1922), featuring Violet Hopson and Clive Brook.

THE MAN WITHOUT DESIRE, Adrian Brunel, GB 1923
Ninna Vanna

THE INFORMER, Arthur Robison, GB 1929
Lars Hanson as Gypo Nolan

J. Stuart Blackton came from America to direct Lady Diana Manners and Victor McLaglen in *The Glorious Adventure* (1922), a tale of the Great Fire of London. This was filmed in Prizmacolour. Herbert Wilcox made a spectacular *Decameron Nights* (1924) in Germany with Werner Krauss, Lionel Barrymore and Ivy Duke. He later made *Dawn* (1928) with Sybil Thorndike as Nurse Cavell. *Woman to Woman* (1922), directed by Graham Cutts with Clive Brook and Betty Compson, was a prestige film for Britain.

THE RING, Alfred Hitchcock, GB 1927
Gordon Harker and Carl Brisson

A COTTAGE ON DARTMOOR, Anthony Asquith, GB 1929
Uno Henning

Many war-time subjects were used. *Zeebrugge* (1924), *Ypres* (1925), *Mons* (1926), *The Somme* (1927) and *The Battles of the Coronel and Falkland Islands* (1927) were a series made by New Era. These were reconstructions which used a great deal of actuality material. But the banner of the documentary film was really to be raised by John Grierson with his *Drifters*, made in 1929.

Alfred Hitchcock, later to become world-famous, began his career in Britain. *The Lodger* (1926), with Ivor Novello, showed his early inclination towards the psychological thriller. *The Ring* (1927) was a boxing story with Carl Brisson, and *The Farmer's Wife* (1929) a charming rural comedy by Eden Philpotts with Lilian Hall-Davis and Jameson Thomas.

Anthony Asquith, much influenced by continental techniques, made *Shooting Stars* (1927), a satire on the film industry. His *Underground* (1928) was a drama of London life and *A Cottage on Dartmoor* (1929) a thriller with Norah Baring, Uno Henning and Hans von Schlettow.

109

When Revolution broke out in Russia in 1917, the cinema discovered a new purpose. It was hailed by Lenin as the greatest of the arts, and this meant propaganda for the new régime. Back from the scenes of bitter fighting came men toughened by experience to record the sufferings of soldiers and the change taking place in the nation's economy. The early films of the Soviets did not seem much different from those of their predecessors, but as systematic study of the cinema, particularly that of Griffith, proceeded, theories like those of Kuleshov were formulated. This culminated in the conception of a dynamic cinema which would move illiterate audiences just as much as intellectual ones. The great tradition of the Russian Theatre with its radical design and

OCTOBER, Sergei Eisenstein, USSR 1928
Kerensky addresses his troops

THE OLD AND THE NEW, Sergei Eisenstein, USSR 1929

brilliant acting was not thrown overboard, but the use of actual people in situations they understood increased, and great stress was laid on effects obtained from the juxtaposition of images. The talent used in the making of films in Russia was enormous and one name stands out above all others. Sergei Eisenstein was born in Riga in 1898. From designing he became a theatre director and in 1924, with the collaboration of Alexandrov, his assistant, and Tisse, his cameraman, made a virtuoso film called *Strike.* In 1925 came *Battleship Potemkin*, the story of a mutiny at Odessa. Wherever it was shown this film caused a furore. Its dynamic editing took full account of the implications of design and movement in each piece of film. The handling of people individually and in groups was remarkable. His next film, *October* (1928), was an impressive reconstruction of the Bolshevik Rising of 1917, and *The Old and the New* (1929) was a study of changing conditions on the land. With Eisenstein the formal presentation was all-important.

111

THE HEIR TO GENGHIS KHAN, Vsevelod Pudovkin, USSR 1928
On the Steppes of Central Asia

The other great figure was the Ukrainian Alexander Dovzhenko, a true visual poet. Beginning with the mystical *Zvenigora* (1928), he then made *Arsenal* (1929) and his masterpiece *Earth* (1930), in which his love of his native Ukraine is expressed with rich imagery and true poetry.

Dziga Vertov was to confine himself to reality, and developed his Kino Eye theories in such films as *One Sixth of the World* (1926), *The Eleventh Year* (1928) and the amusing *Man With the Movie Camera* (1929). Pudovkin, another great talent, made *Mother* (1926), based on Gorki's story, and *The End of St Petersburg* (1927) which is a companion piece to *October*. His finest film, however, is the beautiful *Heir to Jenghis Khan* (1928), shot in central Asia with Valerji Inkishinov in the lead.

The partnership of Kozintsev and Trauberg made *The Cloak* (1926) after Gogol, and *New Babylon* (1928) about the Paris commune. Pudovkin appeared as an actor in this latter film as well as in Otsep's *A Living Corpse* (1929), filmed in Berlin.

Individual films from Russia include: Kuleshov's *By the Law* (1926), based on a Jack London story; *Bed and Sofa* (1927) by Abram Room, a comedy of the housing shortage; *Women of Ryazan* (1927) by Olga Preobrazhenskaia; *Two Days* (1927) by

NEW BABYLON, Kozintsev and Trauberg, USSR 1928
War on the Paris Commune

BED AND SOFA, Abram Room, USSR 1927
Vladimir Fogel and Nicolai Batalov. A Russian Design for Living

AELITA, Protozanov, USSR 1924 ▶

WOMEN OF RYAZAN, Olga Preobrazhenskaia, USSR 1927

Georgi Stabovoi, a drama of civil war in the Ukraine; and *The Girl With the Hatbox* (1927), a comedy by Boris Barnet with Anna Sten. Protozanov, who returned from exile in France, made *Aelita* (1924) with strange futurist settings designed by Alexandra Exter of the Tairov Theatre, and *The Forty-First* (1927). Two fine films of 1929 were Victor Turin's *Turksib*, an epic record of the building of a railroad, and Ermler's *Fragment of an Empire*.

The earliest films to come out of Russia were *Polikuska* (1920) and *The Station Master* (1925), both by Zheliabushsky and featuring the actor Ivan Moskvin. Konstantin Eggert's *Marriage of the Bear* (1926) was also well known outside Russia. The films of Eisenstein, Pudovkin and Dovzhenko ran into difficulties abroad and were only known to minority audiences, but Hollywood was aware of the new standards in the Russian cinema. The growth of the Film Society movement and the appearance of serious film magazines like *Cinea Cine* and *Close Up* helped to make these films known.

After the First World War Hollywood grew in strength. Well-organised film companies like Universal, Paramount, William Fox, First National, Metro-Goldwyn-Mayer absorbed the energies of

MGM Studios at Culver City

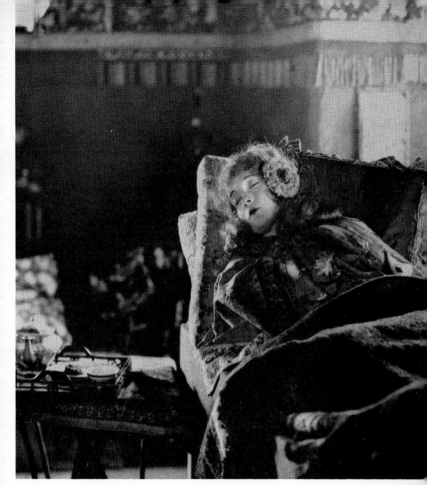

BROKEN BLOSSOMS, D. W. Griffith, USA 1919
Lillian Gish

tycoons such as Carl Laemmle, Jesse Lasky, Adolph Zukor, the Warner Brothers, Marcus Loew, Joseph Schenck and Louis B. Mayer. The big four, D. W. Griffith, Mary Pickford, Douglas Fairbanks and Charles Chaplin, formed their own distributing organisation, United Artists. Before this Griffith had directed his most satisfactory film, *Broken Blossoms* (1919), the sad tale of a Chinaman's love for a terrorised little London waif. The performances of both Lillian Gish and Richard Barthlemess were deeply

TRUE HEART SUSIE, D. W. Griffith, USA 1919
Robert Harron and Lillian Gish

moving. *A Romance of Happy Valley* and *True Heart Susie* of the
same year were idyllic light-weight pieces. In 1920 Griffith made
the first film for United Artists. This was *Way Down East*, a re-
telling of a well-known American melodrama which, by sheer
artistry, he lifted to the highest level, again using the Gish–
Barthlemess team. *Orphans of the Storm* (1922) used the French
Revolution story, and in *America* (1924) Griffith returned to

familiar territory but did not quite achieve the impact of his earlier films. In 1924 he filmed in Germany for *Isn't Life Wonderful*, a study of post-war conditions. He did not make any other film of distinction. The magnitude of his work, however, remains. For many people he was the silent cinema.

Charles Chaplin maintained his hold over audiences, and his films *The Kid* (1920) and *The Pilgrim* (1922) became very popular. His first film for United Artists was, curiously, one in which he did not appear. This was *A Woman of Paris* (1923), a sophisticated drama with Edna Purviance and Adolph Menjou. Back in

A WOMAN OF PARIS, Charles Chaplin, USA 1923
Carl Miller and Edna Purviance, United Artists

comedy he made two brilliant films, *The Gold Rush* (1925) and *The Circus* (1927).

Comedy thrived in America. Buster Keaton, with his solemn abstracted air devoid of a single smile, faced the hard facts of life in *The Navigator* (1924), *Sherlock Jr* (1924) and *The General* (1927). Under the direction of Frank Capra the strange whimsical comedy of Harry Langdon was beautifully realised in *Tramp, Tramp, Tramp* (1926), *The Strong Man* (1926) and *Long Pants* (1927). More brash was the personality of Harold Lloyd, a master of gags in such films as *Safety Last* (1923), *Girl Shy* (1924) and *The Freshman* (1925).

THE CIRCUS, Charles Chaplin, USA 1927 ▶
Charlie Chaplin, United Artists

SEVEN CHANCES, Buster Keaton, USA 1925
Buster Keaton, MGM

Harry Langdon, a sensitive comedian

THE KID BROTHER, Ted Wilde, USA 1927 ▶
Harold Lloyd, Paramount

Erich von Stroheim made his second film, *The Devil's Pass-key*, in 1919. In 1921 came his elaborate and expensive *Foolish Wives*, in which he presented the lives of the idle rich and played his own role as repellingly as he knew how. *Merry-Go-Round* (1922) reverted to his memories of Vienna but, running into trouble, he left Universal for the Goldwyn Company of M.G.M. to make his

THE DEVIL'S PASS-KEY, Erich von Stroheim, USA 1919 ▶
Mae Busch and Maud George, Universal

FOOLISH WIVES, USA 1921 The camera crew, Universal

MERRY-GO-ROUND, Erich von Stroheim, USA 1923
George Hackathorne and Mary Philbin, Universal

masterpiece *Greed* (1923), a savage uncompromising film based on the Frank Norris novel. His forty-reel version was cut to eight, but even in this mutilated form its power is undiminished. For M.G.M. he made one more film, *The Merry Widow* (1925), with the dazzling Mae Murray, but it was far from the spirit of the Lehar operetta, and von Stroheim now moved to Paramount where

GREED, Erich von Stroheim, USA 1923
Von Stroheim directing Cesare Gravina and Dale Fuller. Goldwyn

he made *The Wedding March* (1927) in two parts. Again Viennese life served its maker but again came trouble; *Queen Kelly* (1928) with Gloria Swanson was produced by Joseph Kennedy but was never completed and exists in a version prepared by Miss Swanson. Stroheim had flouted the conventions of Hollywood romance and was never really forgiven.

THE WEDDING MARCH, Erich von Stroheim, USA 1928 ▶
Erich von Stroheim, Paramount

THE CRADLE BUSTER, Frank Tuttle, USA 1922
Glen Hunter and Townsend Martin

SCARAMOUCHE, Rex Ingram, USA 1923
The Massacre of the Swiss Guard,
© Metro Pictures Corporation

THE FOUR HORSEMEN OF THE APOCALYPSE, Rex Ingram,
USA 1921, Alice Terry and Rudolph Valentino,
© Metro Pictures Corporation

Rex Ingram joined the none too steady Metro company in 1919.
In the following year, after making two films, *Shore Acres* and
Hearts are Trumps, he was assigned to *The Four Horsemen of the
Apocalypse* (1921) based on the Ibanez novel of the First World
War. So successful was this film that it launched Rudolph Valen-
tino to a phenomenal success, introduced a new star in Alice
Terry, made Ingram's reputation as a director of distinction and
salvaged the tottering economy of Metro, which was eventually to
be a partner in the M.G.M. set-up. Ingram's subsequent films
were noted for their pictorial beauty and their fine acting: *The
Conquering Power* (1921), again with Valentino and Alice
Terry, *Trifling Women* (1922), *The Prisoner of Zenda* (1922),
Where the Pavement Ends (1923) and *Scaramouche* (1923).
131

THE THREE PASSIONS, Rex Ingram, USA 1927
Andrews Engleman and Alice Terry, United Artists

Tired of the increasing regimentation of Hollywood, Ingram formed his own studio at Nice, where he made his most important film, *Mare Nostrum* (1926), and *The Magician* (1926) and *The Garden of Allah* (1927).

MARE NOSTRUM, Rex Ingram, USA 1926
The execution of the spy, Alice Terry,
© Metro Pictures Corporation

Valentino became a household word and consolidated his position with a series of romantic roles, *The Sheik* (1921), *Blood and Sand* (1922), *Monsieur Beaucaire* (1924) and *The Eagle* (1924). His early death robbed the cinema of a unique personality.

Alla Nazimova came from the Russian Theatre. Her exotic and forceful personality immediately put her into the star class. Her *The Red Lantern* (1919), *Camille* (1921) with Valentino, *A Doll's*

THE REDEEMING SIN, J. Stuart Blackton, USA 1925
Alla Nazimova, Vitagraph

House (1921), *Salome* (1922) and *The Redeeming Sin* (1925), were outstanding.

Mary Pickford continued her *ingénue* roles but also tried costume and modern parts. Her popularity was as great as ever. Her principal films were: *Daddy Long Legs* (1919), *Tess of the Storm Country* (1922), *Rosita* (1923), *Dorothy Vernon of Haddon Hall* (1924), *Little Annie Rooney* (1925) and *Sparrows* (1926).

SALOME, Charles Bryant, USA 1922
Alla Nazimova

Her husband, Douglas Fairbanks, influenced considerably by the German cinema, devised spectacular backgrounds for his athletic prowess in *The Three Musketeers* (1921), *Robin Hood* (1922), *The Thief of Baghdad* (1924), and *The Black Pirate* (1926), the latter in colour.

VANITY FAIR, Hugo Ballin, USA 1923
Otto Matieson as Napoleon

opposite below
ROBIN HOOD, Allan Dwan, USA 1922
The Hall of Nottingham Castle, United Artists

THE THIEF OF BAGDAD, Raoul Walsh, USA 1924
Anna May Wong and Douglas Fairbanks, United Artists

Individual directors made many fine contributions at this time: Henry King with *Tolable David* (1921), *Romola* (1924) and *Stella Dallas* (1925); King Vidor with *The Big Parade* (1925), *La Bohême* (1925) and *The Crowd* (1928); James Cruze with *The Covered Wagon* (1922), *Hollywood* (1923) and *Beggar on Horseback* (1923); Frank Borzage with *Seventh Heaven* (1927);

◀ SEVENTH HEAVEN, Frank Borzage, USA 1927
Janet Gaynor, Fox

THE BIG PARADE, King Vidor, USA 1926, © MGM 1927

THE UNKNOWN, Tod Browning, USA 1927
Lon Chaney and Joan Crawford, © MGM

opposite below

BEGGAR ON HORSEBACK, James Cruze, USA 1925
Edward Everett Horton, Paramount

CAPTAIN BLOOD, David Smith, USA 1923
Vitagraph

SADIE THOMPSON, Raoul Walsh, USA 1928
Gloria Swanson and Lionel Barrymore, United Artists

◀ THE BRIGHT SHAWL, John S. Robertson, USA 1923
Mary Astor and Richard Barthlemess, First National

John Ford with *The Iron Horse* (1924) ; John Stuart Robertson with *Dr Jekyll and Mr Hyde* (1919), *Tess of the Storm Country* (1922) and *The Bright Shawl* (1923) ; Raoul Walsh with *Sadie Thompson* (1928) and T. Hayes Hunter with *Earthbound* (1920) ; Maurice Tourneur with *Prunella* (1919), *Woman* (1919), *Treasure Island* (1920), *Lorna Doone* (1921) and *The Last of the Mohicans* (1922) ; Herbert Brenon with *Peter Pan* (1924), *A Kiss for Cinderella* (1925), *Beau Geste* (1926) and *Sorrell and Son* (1927) ; Clarence Brown with *The Goose Woman* (1924) and *The Flesh and the Devil* (1927) and Paul Fejos with *Lonesome* (1928).

The following leading players should be mentioned: John Gilbert, John Barrymore, Glen Hunter, Antonio Moreno, Charles Farrell, Gareth Hughes, Ramon Novarro, Ronald Colman, Glen Tryon, Wallace Beery, Lon Chaney, and the cowboys Tom Mix, Buck Jones, Hoot Gibson and Harry Carey. Among a formidable array of female stars were Gloria Swanson, Pola Negri, Nazimova, Norma and Constance Talmadge, Mae Murray, Alice Terry, Blanche Sweet, Barbara La Marr, Nita Naldi, Marion Davies, Pauline Frederick and the comediennes Colleen Moore, Bebe Daniels and Laura La Plante.

THE GOLDFISH ▶
Period glamour with Constance Talmadge, 1924 First National

THE WOMAN DISPUTED, Henry King, USA 1928
Norma Talmadge, United Artists

THE TOWER OF LIES, Victor Sjöström, USA 1926
Lon Chaney as the Emperor of Portugallia. © MGM 1925

◀ THE PATRIOT, Ernst Lubitsch, USA 1928
Emil Jannings as Czar Paul, Paramount

The continental influence was much in evidence. Lubitsch and
Pola Negri went their separate ways after *Forbidden Paradise*
(1925), he to make his characteristically stylish comedies: *The
Marriage Circle* (1924), *Three Women* (1924), *Lady Winder-
mere's Fan* (1925) and the dramatic *The Patriot* (1928), again
with Emil Jannings. Victor Sjöström directed Lon Chaney in *He
Who Gets Slapped* (1924) and *Tower of Lies* (1926), and Lillian

Gish and Lars Hanson in *The Scarlet Letter* (1926) and *The Wind* (1928), all of which showed a masterly hand. Mauritz Stiller, who came with Garbo, was not so lucky, but Garbo began her legend in *The Torrent* (1926), *Flesh and the Devil* (1927) and *The Divine Woman* (1927). From Europe also came Dupont, Buchowetzski, Feyder, Pommer, Veidt, Christensen, Paul Fejos, Paul Leni and

◀ THE SCARLET LETTER, Victor Sjöström, USA 1926
Lars Hanson, © MGM

THE WIND, Victor Sjöström, USA 1928
Lillian Gish and Montague Love, © MGM

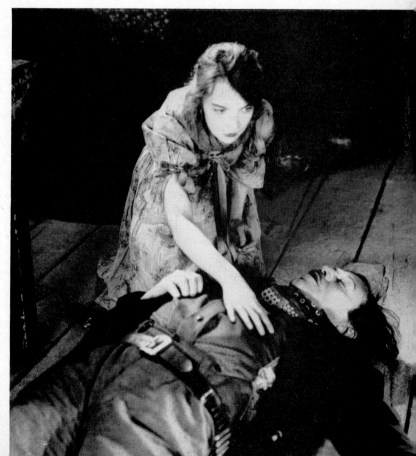

NANOOK OF THE NORTH, Robert Flaherty, USA 1921–22
Nanook, Pathé

Ivan Mosjoukine. The continental influence was best seen in the realistic yet pictorially rich films of Josef von Sternberg: *The Salvation Hunters* (1925), *Underworld* (1927) and *The Docks of New York* (1928). William K. Howard's *White Gold* (1927) particularly reflected the suggestive style of the European directors.

Outside the main stream of cinema stood Roberty Flaherty whose *Nanook of the North*, shot in Baffin land in 1920–22, told the story of an Eskimo Hunter. His *Moana*, filmed in the following

THE DOCKS OF NEW YORK, Josef von Sternberg USA 1928
Baclanova, Paramount

◀ MANSLAUGHTER, Cecil B. de Mille, USA 1922
A typical de Mille scene. Paramount

years, appeared in 1926 and was set in a South Sea Island. He collaborated with F. W. Murnau in *Tabu*, released with music track in 1931, but this film owed more to Murnau than to Flaherty. In *Sunrise* (1927), Murnau achieved one of the most beautiful films made in America.

TABU, F. W. Murnau and Robert Flaherty, USA 1931 ▶
Matahi, Paramount

SUNRISE, F. W. Murnau, USA 1927 Fox

BEN HUR, Fred Niblo, USA 1926
In the Arena. © MGM

Cecil B. de Mille, master of spectacle and exploiter of bathrooms, made *The Ten Commandments* (1923), *The Volga Boatman* (1926) and *King of Kings* (1927). Fred Niblo's *Ben Hur* (1926) must also be recorded.

Epilogue

The silent film had developed rapidly in its creative and industrial aspects but it was doomed. Very early in its career the attempt to make sound films took place and was never lost sight of. On 25th June 1925, Warner Brothers and Western Electric planned to develop sound films. On 6th August 1926, the première of John Barrymore's *Don Juan*, with synchronised music and shorts featuring famous musicians of the day, gave the audience a foretaste of things to come. The première of Al Jolson's *The Jazz Singer* on 6th October 1927, in which he sang and spoke one classic line, 'You aint heard nothin' yet folks. Listen to this', saw a revolution in progress. The Fox Company fell into line and in the same month the first sound newsreel was launched. From synchronised discs the movies went on to sound-on-film and very rapidly technical excellence was achieved.

New faces appeared, older players retired, but generally speaking it is remarkable how many directors adapted themselves to the new medium with its emphasis on speech, sound and music. Visually the new medium recovered its sweep but it was not the same thing as the silent cinema. True, some films were still to be made silent—Mikhail Romm's *Boule de Suif* (1934), Richard Massingham's rich comedies *Tell Me if it Hurts* (1934), *And So to Bed* (1936), the experimental films of Maya Deren (1943) and Shindo's *The Island* (1962), but they were the exception.

A special unique art had perished but was remembered with affection and pride by those who lived through it. It would have been forgotten completely by the people who created it if, in 1935, film archives had not come into existence to preserve for posterity what could be salvaged from the ruins of time, and to ensure that the sound film did not meet a similar fate.

Acknowledgements

I wish to express my thanks to Miss Norah Traylen and Miss Betty Leese, of the stills department of the National Film Archive, and to the James Anderson Memorial Collection.

To the following film companies for the use of their stills: Metro-Goldwyn-Mayer, Paramount Pictures, Svensk Filmindustri, Twentieth Century Fox, United Artists, Universal-International, Universum Film Aktiengesellschaft, Warner Brothers, and to all other film companies whose stills are represented in this book.

Index of actors, directors and producers